Tales of Fishing and Fishermen

Tales of Fishing and Fishermen

James Fyfe

LOCHAR PUBLISHING · MOFFAT · SCOTLAND

© James Fyfe, 1991
Published by Lochar Publishing Limited
MOFFAT DG10 9ED

British Library Cataloguing in Publication Data
Fyfe, James
Tales of fishing and fishermen
I Title
799.12

ISBN 0-948403-87-X

Typeset in 10pt on 11pt Palitino
by Origination, Dunstable, Beds.
and printed by BPCC Wheatons Ltd.

Contents

Preface

IN MORE THAN half-a-century of fishing for salmon and trout I have met a considerable number of colourful characters from all classes of society, people for whom angling is, or was, a way of life – in fact for some of them the be-all and end-all of their existence. This I have tried to reflect in these tales, some of them from yesteryear, when influences such as mass media, with their stulifying effects on the development of personality, were much less powerful and there seemed to be many more interesting individuals around than there are today.

I hope the combination of the humorous and the serious will help the reader to enjoyably while away some of those late autumn and winter nights when the season is closed and we are all anticipating the one which lies ahead; also, that some of the information contained in the stories may be useful to those who return home all too often with an empty creel.

My thanks are due to my wife, Kathleen, for the patience she showed and the help she gave while I was compiling the manuscript, and also to my son Cameron for his valuable suggestions.

J.F.

P.S. I would also like to thank Sandy Leventon, Editor of the magazine *Trout and Salmon,* for allowing me to include in the collection '2000+AD', which appeared in the April, 1990 issue; and David Goodchild, Editor of *Salmon Trout & Sea-Trout,* for giving me permission to use 'Piscatorial Bliss?', which was published in that magazine in April, 1991.

Hooked – and Landed

SOME MEN are obsessed by golf, some by cars, some by bridge, some perhaps by the Devil. In Derek Robert's case it was rod and line which shaped his life-pattern and, to a certain extent, moulded his character. His mania meant his sights were set on one target and one target only and he was willing to go to almost any extreme to hit the bull bang in the middle.

In his early forties and a college lecturer in Aberdeen, he was quite a handsome fellow, slightly rugged, highly articulate, of charming personality; but rendered perhaps a little self-centred by his years of celibacy. He had always spent his long vacations – and they *were* long – fishing for salmon on practically all the outstanding waters of the North and West, wherever permission could be purchased. But, growing a little tired of writing out numerous applications each year and having to keep an accurate and detailed timetable to see when he was due where, of having to sacrifice valuable time driving when he should have been fishing, of plying his rod on stretches which he did not know as well as he would have wished, setting great store as he did on an intimate knowledge of the water, he finally decided that what he needed was an excellent beat of his very own. However, he wasn't the first angler who had cherished such hopes and found them impossible to realise on being quoted the incredibly large sums required. He wanted nothing but the very best and had no interest in anything that was even a very good second class. And, living as he did in Aberdeen, there was only one river within feasible travelling distance that offered the excellence he demanded. Often his working day was of short duration, so, even during term-time, he would be able to fish almost to his heart's content if he could only realise his ambition and gain unrestricted access to a stretch of that incomparable stream...

But although well paid for his intellectual labours and by no means a spendthrift, apart from his huge bill for fishing dues, he found it impossible even to remotely approach the vast figures demanded for beats as they came on to the market.

He racked his brains for a solution - and found a way, desperate, perhaps, but one which had at least a small chance of success. He could at least try.

During the close-season – it was the Christmas holidays in fact – he made a tour of many of the hostelries lying between Aberdeen and a point about 50 miles to the west, engaging in conversation those barmen and customers who were willing to chat about the local beats and their owners.

Patient and exhaustive enquiries, sometimes rendered more productive by the incentive of the "cratur", revealed only one obvious possibility. Her name was Penelope Symington-Croe, a syllabic combination which, on hearing it for the first time, made him shudder. Apparently she was the epitome of the proverbially frustrated spinster, eager for permanent male

company – which was fine - but also highly distrustful of any suitors and convinced that, if zealous anglers, they were interested only in the piscatorial rather than the matrimonial amenities she had to offer. She would enter into no liaison on such terms and was determined that the man she married, if such a miracle were ever to come about, would want her for herself or not at all - a condition which, as it happened, cut her chances to a level that could only be described as abysmal.

Fearing the worst and on asking what she looked like, he was simply told he would not fail to recognise her.

He also learned that apart from two servants she lived quite alone - both her parents having passed on - in an ancestral home bearing a suitably aristocratic name. And that, no doubt, she would be attending a 'cheese and wine' being held in a riverside village hall one evening the following week...

He bought himself a ticket.

Although he had maintained the state of bachelorhood for so long, Roberts was not entirely immune to the charms of the opposite sex. And so, when confronted with the shapeless and stony-faced Miss Symington-Croe, he immediately dismissed attempted implementation of his plan as out of the question. After all, there were certain limits, one had to keep things in perspective and retain a sense of propriety. There was no point in drinking nectar if, when you got home, you had to swill down a huge gulp of gall . . .

He had one glass of wine and departed.

But a further walk, a few weeks later, by that enchanting stretch of salmon-rich water, now tenanted by early springers which occasionally crashed tantalisingly to the surface, made him start to swither once more, weakening his resolution to steer well clear.

To Hell with it, he would investigate again. After all, it was true, cliché or not, that beauty didn't go very deep. Perhaps she had other assets, unknown to or undetected by those who knew her only superficially. And free and untrammelled access to water like that was bound to compensate for a lot of her shortcomings.

The next time it was a meeting for 'environmentalists'. A discussion followed the talk, and Roberts hastened to introduce himself, ostensibly to express his whole-hearted approval of a point she had made to the speaker. She was slightly more affable and less repellant than her forbidding countenance suggested, but not much, and, each time he considered her as his life-partner he was overcome by what was no less than a feeling of sheer panic, laced with revulsion. He knew he would not have looked at her twice - nay, he would have turned hurriedly away - if his main concern had been for a spouse. But his mind's eye kept drifting back to that glittering mile of water, to that absolute mecca of a salmon stream . . .

Hooked – and Landed

No more than half-heartedly he suggested another meeting - for dinner - and Miss Symington-Croe smiled as sweetly as her physiognomy allowed. And accepted.

While they strolled by the river one day sometime later he gave her surreptitiously to understand that his sole pastimes were linguistic research and photography and asked, rather disinterestedly, what kind of fish the water held. The subject of angling was never mentioned, and he never gave the game away.

They say one can learn to put up with anything in time, especially if stakes are involved and they are high enough, and after a few months Roberts considered himself more or less prepared to take the marital plunge. It was still a high price to pay, but the reward, he reckoned, was just enough to make it viable. Anyway, he convinced himself, what he was cementing was a fishing rather than a conjugal contract.

Penelope accepted, outwardly unemotionally, perhaps somewhat uncomprehendingly, a proposal which she thought would never come her way - marriage to a man, a handsome, well educated man who was not river-daft.

A fortnight's honeymoon was spent in Brittany. Roberts got through it somehow, consoling himself at the worst moments with the intoxicating thoughts of the reward he would shortly reap.

"God," he asked himself, "is it really worth it?"

But he had made his bed.

On taking up residence with Mrs. Penelope Symington-Croe Roberts at The Turrets he let things go along quietly, impatient as he was, until the beginning of his summer vacation, then inadvertently mentioned one evening that he had had a stroll by the river and been quite entranced as he watched an angler hook and play a salmon. He had in fact been observing this sort of thing for some time and went on to say that during these long vacations he often found time weighed heavily on his hands. He thought he would "get himself a rod" and see if he liked it.

Penelope, perhaps more shapeless than ever, stood there in all her glory, her expression one of fiery belligerence, her chubby, upturned lips and her irregular teeth set in their acre of gum in that great leaden face which itself had all the attractions of a lunar landscape.

She told him he had better find some other outlet. Knowing he wasn't interested in the delicate art she had sold the entire rights not long before their wedding.

"But never mind," she added, "you've always got me!"

Once Bitten . . .

HAVING A LEAN SEASON, an empty deep-freeze, and desperate for a handsome fish to enhance both table and atmosphere for the party the following evening, Alastair Hill was on the water at first light. Although neither he nor Joan ever ate salmon themselves, preferring white fish, he was very conscious of the fact that each and every one of their friends adored it, expected it, and would be disappointed if denied it.

But then they did not understand about droughts and over-netting, about the deadly disease called Ulcerative Dermal Necrosis and poor, irregular runs. So quite unthinkable was the thought that he couldn't supply the usual prime specimen in all its silver and rose-pink glory.

He laboured on without success and, as the sun began to shake itself free of the surrounding hillocks and copses and to climb unmolested into the sky, casting its ever brighter and destructive rays over the gin-clear water, he decided that the turbulent Geyser might offer a last, slim chance.

When he reached the head of the stream he stopped in his tracks, his attention arrested by the sight of a beautifully-proportioned salmon of about 10lb lying at the edge of the pool, partly submerged and obviously quite dead. He lifted it out.

The fish looked daisy-fresh. Why it had succumbed he had no idea, but he tried to convince himself that an otter, disturbed by him before it had the opportunity to breakfast on its favourite morsel just behind the head, had been responsible. But a close inspection revealed neither tooth nor claw marks.

It then occurred to him that the salmon could have been the victim of poachers using the most unscrupulous and unhygienic of methods, but was inclined to reject this possibility as its eyes were quite unglazed and its gills were devoid of any blue tinge - unmistakable signs, he had heard, of cymag poisoning. Bending over his find, he scrutinized it, smelt it, prodded it, and even made an incision with his penknife to check the colour and texture of the flesh. Both were exactly as they should have been.

He concluded that the creature had only just expired. It was in no way contaminated or diseased and, in the circumstances, it would have been sheer folly not to have taken it.

"Joan!" he called, as soon as he entered the house. "Look at this! Isn't it a beauty? Just the thing for the party!"

Joan, in total agreement, praised her husband for his achievement, adding that a whole salmon always gave a party that extra "something".

When it came to culinary decoration his wife was as accomplished an artist as he was reputedly a skilled angler, and at seven o'clock on the Saturday evening the dining-room at 12 Benbecula Drive was the scene of a mouth-watering display, with pride of place going to the salmon - cooked to perfection and with head and tail removed - which lay on a huge platter, surrounded by sprigs of cress, slices of cucumber and tomato, crisp, green lettuce and small succulent radishes, and flanked by two plates of home-baked bread and four bottles of a not unrenowned vintage wine. Everything was there to satisfy the requirements of the most fastidious gourmet.

Then, a few minutes before half-past seven, a loud shriek brought Alastair running downstairs to find Joan standing at the table, her hands clasped to her face.

"Look," she sobbed, "at what Toby has done. The middle, too. He's just jumped out of the window. I knew he was out in the garden but I thought the window was shut."

Toby was their big tom.

"Now, there's no need to upset yourself," consoled Alastair. "Let's see what we can do."

A few minutes' work with a long, sharp knife put paid to the holed and ruffled centre section and when the two parts were pushed together the most perspicacious fuss-pot could hardly have detected the slightest blemish or suspected that a good half-pound of flesh was missing.

The guests arrived, emitting their "Oohs" and their "Aahs", sincere for the most part, on beholding the magnificent spread concocted for their gastronomic pleasure. Alastair received congratulatory pats on the back and the odd: "I wish my husband would go out and learn to catch fish like that - all he does is lose golf balls!"

The greater part of the salmon duly disappeared down a dozen appreciative throats, well lubricated by a wine whose bouquet seemed to have been admirably engineered to create the happiest of liaisons with the unique flavour of salmon. Alastair complimented himself on his good fortune at a time when failure had loomed large - and on the good sense he had shown in taking the fish instead of leaving it for the scavengers of the riverbank.

So ended a well nigh perfect social evening. When all their friends had gone a dutiful husband helped his wife to tidy and wash up. Then he said he would smoke a quiet pipe in the garden before turning in.

On opening the french window he stopped, his pipe forgotten. Toby was lying rigid on the step. He picked him up and found he was quite dead.

It was only when he carried the cat inside that the frightening possibilities struck him. As casually as he could he mentioned to Joan that they had better take precautionary steps - just to be on the safe side, just in case the salmon had been the culprit. Needless to say he kept a certain item of information to himself, otherwise his wife's anxiety would have fast become panic,

Sweating profusely he picked up the telephone and dialled the Infirmary.

They took the names and addresses of all the guests, who were unceremoniously dragged from bed by the police and, shocked into wakefulness, were driven post-haste to the hospital, where they each underwent a rigorous examination. All the results were negative.

The Hills finally got to sleep just after four o'clock and when Alastair went out to bury Toby about midday their neighbour, Johnny Grant, came over to the garden fence:

"Oh, Alastair, I knew you were throwing a party last night and I saw no point in spoiling your evening so I just put Toby on your back doorstep. He ran right in front of me out there in the street and I just couldn't stop in time. I'm awfully sorry".

The Big Catch

JOHN ALLERDYCE, C.A., had worked hard every night at the office for weeks, and now that the pressure was off he reckoned he deserved a break, and decided to spend a whole night on the river.

He arrived at the Corner Pool a little before 10 o'clock on one of those balmy midsummer evenings, when the day's combination of hot sun and low water usually signify ideal fishing conditions after dark.

The accountant sat down on the bank to enjoy the pleasant surroundings and passed the time with a cup of tea from his flask and a long satisfying pipe of tobacco. He observed the living things around him - the parr and fingerlings snapping at tiny flies in the shallows, the mallard which swept past low and fast, the dipper which flirted playfully from rock to rock - and he felt happy and relaxed, far from the mad whirling world of figures and telephones and typewriters.

In fact as the light began to fade he felt more at one with the world than he had done for some time. His thoughts strayed nostalgically to previous successes with the sea trout, especially big fish, and he looked forward to enjoying similar sport that very night.

It was not long before he was casting his favourite trio of Grey Monkey, Peter Ross and White Moth over the deep and gentle cant which was generally recognised as one of the best lies on the entire beat.

Then came the first tentative tug, followed by a vicious, full-blooded pull. His reel screamed as if in agony and he found himself battling with a trout which was obviously well above average size. He finally pulled it on to the shingle and could see that it weighed at least 4lb.

In again. And hardly had he got set when another huge fish tore at his fly and went off in a jet-propelled run. But he tamed it, just as he had done the first one, and soon it lay beside its lesser mate in the bottom of his large creel.

He just could not go wrong. The third sea trout he hooked jumped right out of the water and landed beside his basket. This promised to be the best night he had ever had. Dared he hope for more?

Hope or not, the incredible slaughter went on. The sea trout were really committing suicide, throwing themselves with gay abandon at one or other of his flies. He was now almost bound to have a catch which would remain a record for all time, certainly for this if not for any river, and any doubts about achieving it were finally dispelled when, after a long and hectic fight, he dragged out the queen of them all - a great, thickset hen sea trout which scaled at least 10lb.

It was his twenty-second fish of the night. The silvery monsters lay packed thick to the brim of his creel and piled high on the stones all around it.

13

*   *   *

He awoke with a start, stiff as a board and chilled to the marrow. The sun had been up a good hour and was already casting its dazzling, midsummer rays on the clear water of the Corner Pool, where a small sea trout splashed belatedly in the tail.

In the tree above his head a thrush sang out loud and crisp and clear.

Or was it a mocking-bird?

2000+AD

THE GOSPEL, preached so fervently by so many for so long, that the whole natural environment was a gift to be cherished and protected, had been whole-heartedly endorsed by the populace at large by the beginning of the twenty-first Century. The next logical step was the demand that as a national asset, every single square inch of it, and each of the numerous leisure pursuits it offered, be made available to one and all. Nothing was to be denied to anyone.

The angling fraternity did not hesitate to join the fray and its numbers, which had grown from some four millions in the late eighties to almost double that figure by the first decade of the new century, began to make their voices heard in town squares and public halls everywhere. The exponents of rod and line closed their ranks to a man, or woman, and their demand was as unambiguous as it was absolute: common access to all the waters of the land, including the rich and hallowed salmon rivers and lochs of the North and West. Not a single one, or any part of it, was to be out of bounds.

A somewhat surprised Government at first reacted, or at least appeared to react, as if the whole thing deserved to be treated as a mere joke. The politicians had survived equally hare-brained demands in other spheres and this one, vociferous and widespread as it was, would, given time, lose its momentum and fizzle out like all the others. When the anglers let it be known that they were in anything but a jocular mood and proved it by banding themselves in their hundreds of thousands into a new body which called itself Anglers' Liberation, those sitting in Westminster then condescended to treat the matter a little more seriously and explained that while the request for right of access everywhere for the purpose of bird-watching or hill-walking, or simply for a country stroll, was one thing, a *carte blanche* to angle for the lordly salmon on those superlative waters which were so safe and secure in the hands of a civilised few was something altogether different. That would be sacrilege and vilification of a valuable national heritage. While the politicians apparently did not appreciate the hypocritical and contradictory nature of their cliché the anglers' leaders did so in a flash and did not fail to make the most of it.

And when the Government, having finally realised that the demand was a genuine one all right, pronounced it to be quite unattainable and not even worthy of discussion, Anglers' Liberation, which had trebled its following in a matter of weeks, decided that the time was ripe for positive action.

Nurtured as they had been from an early age on the concept that force and blackmail and, if need be, violence, rarely misfired as profitable means to profitable ends where hitherto intractable administrations were concerned, provided that demonstrations were conducted on a massive scale and

Tales of Fishing and Fishermen

bolstered by the full TV and press coverage which they inevitably attracted, the fishermen were not slow to answer the call to arms. Determined as they had become to blast the whole unjust structure to its very foundations, which alone would satisfy them, they paraded, on AL's word of command, at various mustering points throughout the length and breadth of the country and boarded coaches which deposited them, armed to the hilt with rods, nets and all, in undisciplined hordes on private estates in every corner of the land. Having driven the knife home they gave the blade a vicious twist by paying particular attention to such sacrosanct streams as Laxford and Dionard, Oykel and Inver, Dee and Spey. The tranquility that had reigned there for centuries was suddenly subjected to a degree of disturbance which had more than a few lairds turning in their graves and seemed likely to drive many more into theirs.

And that was just the beginning. As the incursions on to forbidden territory became ever longer and more frequent a state of piscatorial anarchy developed. It became obvious to all that the frustration and resentment which had built up amongst anglers over the years in a supposedly socialised society was to be assuaged by nothing else than the removal of the outrageous privilege enjoyed by only a tiny minority, by nothing less than the granting of the right to every individual to fish all waters, loch or stream, fresh or salt, here, there and everywhere.

A somewhat jittery government now adopted a more acquiescent attitude, guardedly promising some sort of change in the system, but it was faced with a rank and file long accustomed to the devious ways of its rulers and was peremptorily given twelve months to "put matters right", it being clearly explained exactly what these words meant. Otherwise the invasion would increase tenfold and all hell would be let loose. The hook had been driven well and truly home and the hands holding the rod had no intention of releasing their grip . . .

Even the most obstinate of the political bosses were now convinced that further delay would only provoke further trouble, and it wasn't long before a host of compulsory purchase orders were reluctantly prepared and served on all the landlords, absent and present, whose forefathers, back in a dim and often questionable past, had, at best, been granted the fishing rights and properties as recompense for some deed of doubtful worth, or, at worst, had simply seized them, said they were theirs, and handed them down the line.

So all the private waters of the land and everything that went with them were evaluated at a figure which ran into billions and which would be taken from the national coffers to fill, even fuller than they already were, those of the unfortunates who had been so cruelly deprived of the unique treasures they and theirs had enjoyed from time immemorial. But this intended act of misplaced generosity elicited a further seething onslaught by Anglers' Liberation: those thieves and imposters, the last remnants of an odious plutocratic system, should consider themselves lucky in having held on to their ill-gotten gains for so long, so why in heaven's name should they be compensated for losing something which was never rightfully theirs in the first place? You don't pay robbers for returning what they have stolen. No, the moneys would be re-channelled for the benefit of the nation's anglers. They would go towards the conversion of the castles and the stately manors into "Anglers' Centres", equipped with all the paraphernalia savoured up till then only by a chosen few: drying rooms, rod rooms, private lockers, deep freezes, angling films, casting tuition and meals of the quality the kitchens had produced for the tables of the previous occupants.

But the Government, having consulted its appropriate departments, was advised of the potential dangers and insisted that large sums would also be required to implement a regular and widespread restocking policy - with which AL's Executive were in total agreement - which involved the building and staffing of countless hatcheries. The Centres, too, would be costly to manage and, in order to safeguard the high standard of the fishings, a huge army of wardens would have to be employed so that rivers were not soon ruined by unscrupulous characters, of whom, they suspected, there was more than the odd one in the ranks of the angling fraternity. Accordingly, those found to be angler-poachers and convicted of malpractices - using illegal tackle or using tackle illegally - would be heavily fined and forced to relinquish their right to fish for five years on a first conviction, for ten years on a second and for ever if they broke the rules a third time. The threat of such extreme forms of chastisement brought howls of anguish from the enlightened, from those who had been reared in the belief that miscreants were miscreants through no fault of their own. But their leaders were more practical in their thinking and finally won the day, albeit with a struggle. They were well aware that unless stringent measures were enforced the bonanza might be of short duration and that they could end up being no better-off fishing-wise than they had been before.

The anglers were then informed that, to defray the enormous running costs of the new set-up, the price of the annual national licence, in the first instance, would be £500. For this sum (an average weekly wage in the new century and accepted by all but the dullest among them as a reasonable outlay for the splendid amenity offered) they could now have what they had long dreamed of - a passport to any water in the land, where they could use any legitimate lure or bait, at any time, Sundays included.

At last the great day came and an endless procession of caravans, motorised homes and tent-filled trailers created an influx of Klondike proportions into all the best fishing areas and the far North-West in particular - that mecca of salmon-packed streams set in a landscape of incomparable beauty - was immediately subjected to a piscatorial rat race that turned its peaceful acres into a raucous arena. The hitherto unsullied air echoed with harsh invective and blasphemy as those impatient for success hurried and scurried to be first into the most promising-looking pools and feuds became the order of the day. In no time at all salmon and sea trout were being slaughtered in hundreds, then in thousands, many of them by blatant foul-hooking in those rivers of small dimensions but large abundance. Waters were raped and declined to such an extent within four or five years that a considerable percentage of the newly-privileged, determined to get something for their money, indulged in even more base misdemeanours of every conceivable kind. The greed and selfishness of which they had accused the disinherited was but nothing compared to their own. They even formed themselves into bands, wardens did likewise and bloody battles ensued; and the vast army of watch-dogs, their strength already diminished through resignations, was not nearly vast enough. They simply could not cope.

As stocks continued to decrease at calamitous speed, so did the number of those willing to fork out the money for the piece of paper which they had always believed would be an open sesame to an anglers' Utopia. Gradually the Anglers' Centres closed and fell into disrepair.

What had been a piscatorial paradise for the few had become a piscatorial desert for the many and none of the latter was any longer interested in once prolific salmon rivers which were now more barren than the overfished public waters to which they had been earlier confined. Hence, there was no opposition when former proprietors were invited, by a shame-faced government, to return. This they did, re-acquiring both rights and mansions from an administration which appeared both relieved and delighted to be shorn of ownership.

Peace also returned and, slowly but surely, did the salmon.

Impasse

Bailiff Danny McSpadden decided one glorious autumn morning to devote rather more attention than normal to the long and exclusive Inchcarlachan beat of the mighty salmon river of which he regularly patrolled several miles. Inchcarlachan, whose endless succession of enticing streams and pools and almost total lack of unfishable water led one to wonder why its Creator had looked so magnanimously upon those destined to own it, was without doubt the most rewarding stretch between source and sea, and was therefore in great demand despite the high charges, and jealously guarded. In fact, the fees had that year been raised to £40 per day, £220 per week and £8,000 for the season and, vigilant as was the collective eye kept on this hallowed water by the higher-grade employees of the estate hierarchy, the proprietor was keen that McSpadden, representing officialdom, should be seen on it frequently, vaguely promising him some sort of vague reward if he did so.

New faces were always to be seen on the water, especially tourists on day and weekly tickets and the canny Laird of Inchcarlachan meant to take no chances with *arrivistes* who, in the more acceptable society of yesteryear would never have indulged in the aristocratic pastime of salmon fishing, let alone plied their rods on sacrosanct beats such as his. Their presence there was costing them aplenty, even allowing for their new-found affluence, and if sport did not come up to the standard they expected, who could be sure to what base misdemeanours they might not descend?

Also, it was strongly suspected that some weekly and season licence-holders were sub-letting their permits to desperate visitors at £60-£70 per day, so that rogue anglers were appearing too frequently, a problem which inspired the insertion of yet another clause on an already rule-ridden permit. It was pointed out in no uncertain language that tickets were strictly non-transferable and that any holder failing to observe this regulation would immediately forfeit his right to fish. And there would be no refund, not even a single penny.

One season-permit had been issued in the name of Andrew Bonner who, with his identical twin brother, Malcolm, had taken up residence in the nearby town the previous December. The Bonners had become joint owners of the huge, recently-built Strathlachan Hotel and, on confirming soon after their arrival the great cost of the fishing as well as its high quality, had created the impression throughout the neighbourhood, quietly and subtly, that, in spite of constant overtures from Andrew, Malcolm detested venturing forth with rod and line as much as his brother loved it.

In actual fact, they were angling addicts both, their passion for the sport equalled only by their burning desire to fill their coffers with gold, so they were not slow to see that the situation offered, at one and the same time, extra financial gain coupled with endless months of exhilarating pleasure. The writing of a cheque for £8,000 rankled more than a little, but, on the other hand, they were in an exceptional position, fate having decreed that they should look alike as two salmon ova.

Consequently, the clause about the non-transfer of tickets, and the penalty for non-observance thereof, so conspicuously printed in heavy black type, did not, they reckoned, hold any fears for them. Each twin spent three days each week on the river and three in the hotel. In other words, while one fished, the other worked, and vice-versa.

But they took every conceivable precaution to ensure that their stratagem went on smoothly and unchallenged. While on the water, they wore identical outer garments - in fact they were often the same garments. They always carried maximum-range walkie-talkies in their ample fishing bags and, in a breast pocket, a small cassette-recorder to pick up any riverside conversations held with officials or other anglers, just in case the twin due to fish the next day should make a fatal slip. And because even holders of "seasons" (all of whom were personally known both to Bailiff McSpadden and senior staff on the estate), had to carry their permits at all times, Malcolm had a facsimile of Andrew's.

Anyone remarking to Malcolm that he seemed to work while Andrew played received the reasonably convincing reply that he himself had quite a pleasant task and enjoyed wandering about the hotel during the day, just keeping a general eye on things, while his brother spent each and every evening doing all the tiring administrative work. Moreover, the arrangement suited Malcolm who was, he admitted in a tone tinged with guilt and with an apologetic smile, as addicted to the TV screen as his brother was to the wand.

The Bonners successfully practised this admirably engineered ploy for weeks on end. Skilled and resolute anglers both, their huge deep-freezes in the hotel kitchens were kept full to the brim in spite of the heavy inroads made upon them as the holiday season progressed. In fact, they purchased two more. Apart from the revenue culled from the well-to-do guests, they also ran a restaurant which became highly popular with passing tourists who gulped down choice salmon steaks by the hundred and took even more away in sandwiches.

So profits and monthly statements grew and grew, so much so that it was decided a wiser policy to put less in the bank and more in the strong-box in a secluded loft high in the left wing.

The brothers reckoned that by mid-June they had recouped almost the entire outlay of £8,000; that some time between then and the end of August, a period during which salmon runs were quite phenomenal both in size and frequency, they would be crying quits; and that thereafter (until the season ended on October 31), it would be all clear profit. So there was much smacking of lips and rubbing of hands and projects for expansion and extended winter holidays far from the damp chill of a Highland glen.

But, for one of those mysterious reasons, the teeming shoals of July did not appear and the expected bonanza was not realised. Then the runs started to build up in August, to such an extent that nature seemed to be regretting her lapse during the previous month and was determined to redress the balance. From vantage points such as Boulder Bridge, the salmon could be seen lying in tiers. The river was literally chock-a-block with this silvery harvest which had surged in from the sea.

But a harvest is there to be reaped and the twins, victims like so many of their fellows of that common human frailty which fails to recognise that a pot of gold and a mountain of the stuff are much the same thing, decided that two full rods would make up the leeway sooner than one, that duties could be delegated and the hotel run adequately well without either of them for a day or two each week. Each would fish an extreme end of the beat and, if Lady Luck continued to walk with them, no one would know the truth for long enough, perhaps never. In other words, a previously almost infallible dodge was now replaced with a machination that was fraught with danger.

So back to that early autumn morning.

"Hello there, Mr. Bonner!"

Andrew looked up from his casting over the High Rock Pool to see McSpadden crunching his way over the gravel "By God, there's some fish," the Bailiff continued, "how many have you got, Mr. Bonner?"

Andrew pointed to the salmon lying in a depression a few yards from the water's edge. "There's six there already, biggest about 14 lb."

"Aye sir, it's a grand run. I've never seen one quite like it, even on this river. I'll take a walk downstream to see if there's anyone else fishing. You would expect them to be out in force today. You'll probably end up with about a score o' them. Good day to you, sir."

The Bonners were quite prepared for such an eventuality and as soon as the bailiff was out of sight and earshot Andrew called up his brother on the walkie-talkie to tell him that McSpadden was on his way. "Hard to say how long you can safely stay. Depends on how long he spends chatting to other anglers. I've got six, by the way."

"Damn it," answered his brother, "I've got seven and just hooked another now. It's not a big fish, so I'll get it out and clear off. Should be away with plenty of time to spare. Over and out."

Only minutes after McSpadden had left Andrew, an estate jeep, electrically powered and specially constructed for negotiating rough terrain, drew alongside the bailiff.

"Jump aboard!" invited the head keeper, "I'm trying this thing out for the

Tales of Fishing and Fishermen

Laird before we commit ourselves to a purchase. I'll run you down to the bottom end and drop you off there if you like. You can tell me what you think of it."

"Fine," replied the bailiff, "I intended walking down but I'll walk back up. It's all the same."

"Can't get over that steep ridge, I'm afraid, not even with this thing," said the keeper as they neared the last pool of the Inchcarlachan beat. "I'll drop you here before I turn round."

"Just grand. Seems a useful buggy, Angus, but I think you would need a pretty strong stomach to run about in it all day! Cheerio!"

Keeper and bailiff went off in different directions, the former back into the heart of the estate, the latter towards the heart of the Silver Pot.

Malcolm was preparing to beach what had been an extra-lively seven or eight-pounder when McSpadden stepped forward, his face revealing at first bewilderment, then comprehension, and finally open hostility. The hotelier, beholding in front of him about the very last person he at that moment wanted to see, was nonplussed and allowed the salmon to run round a protruding rock, thrash about and escape.

The bailiff challenged Malcolm almost gloatingly:

"I don't know whether you're Andrew Bonner or Malcolm Bonner, but I do know that only one of you has a permit and that both of you are fishing."

Malcolm, completely disorientated by the fact that McSpadden had arrived at the Silver Pot so soon after the warning from his brother, made a great effort to rally himself and retorted in a voice which did not reflect the discomfort he felt:

"I'm Andrew Bonner and here is my permit." He held it in front of McSpadden's eyes. "Satisfied?"

The bailiff stamped off, then ran, so impatient was he to get back to the top of the beat and the other twin, who would be ticketless and, therefore, without defence.

But Andrew, warned in turn by Malcolm over the latter's walkie-talkie, was back in the hotel by the time a very puffed McSpadden had reached the High Rock.

McSpadden cursed himself for not having asked the first twin for his permit. For he now knew that there was no action that could be taken. He could prove nothing.

Certainly, he had gained a sort of half-victory in so far as he had put an end to the days when both twins appeared on the river. They would not try that again. But the other half belonged to the Bonners, since it was quite impossible for anyone to tell which of them was fishing, for only Andrew and Malcolm knew which was Andrew and which was Malcolm.

Booze and the Beast

LAST SUMMER certain parts of Scotland, and the Central Highlands in particular, were subjected to an extraordinary invasion when a terrible trio from the great industrial conurbation of South-East Lancashire, none other than Fred Tunstall, Horace Hickinshaw and "Porky" Towey, three rollicking adventurers renowned throughout their own airt for their incredible escapades on canal, quarry and in waterside taverns, decided for once to cast themselves clear of their native haunts and go on a fishing and drinking spree far to the north, to a region which, they had heard, was in keeping with their own unrestrained temperaments, where both rod and tankard could be enjoyed to the full. They were coarse fishers all, and aptly designated as such, because their gear would have been more appropriate in the savage waters of the tropics, 'midst ferocious shark and marlin, than amongst the more manageable fish of the inland waters of home. Their methods likewise.

As ignorant of the geography of remote Caledonia as they were of their own homeland, they set off with an ancient wooden caravan in tow and a small boat on the roof of their complaining old roadster. Someone told them to get on to the M6 and to keep going. This they did but, unfortunately, they were on the wrong carriageway and covered a total of 100 useless miles before learning at a services station that they had been travelling south instead of north. The sun that had blazed in their eyes had meant nothing as a navigational aid.

However, they finally succeeded in sorting themselves out and proceeded as planned, passing their starting point hours later with nothing to show for their endeavours but beer-filled bellies.

"Porky" had heard vaguely of Loch Ken, that it was somewhere in Scotland, and by sheer good luck they asked about it at Tebay and were told to leave the A74 after Carlisle and to take the so-called Euroroute (A75) via Dumfries and Castle Douglas. But, since this complicated itinerary was met with triple, uncomprehending stares, the AA patrolman advised them to get behind a big truck marked "Northern Ireland Deliveries" and to follow it as far as Castle Douglas, then to take the road to New Galloway, along which they could not fail to see Loch Ken on their left. He hoped they would not end up in Stranraer, or even Larne.

They got there eventually, without too many detours.

They caught pike in Loch Ken, including one of 21^1/$_2$ lb., and they caught pike in Loch Awe upon which, journeying further north, they had come upon by chance rather than design. Their appetites whetted for more isolated and hence perhaps even more rewarding areas, they pushed onwards, clattering over Connel Ferry and moving through Benderloch with their largely home-made, bone-shaking contraption which objected more and more as they hauled it further and further into the heart of the Highlands.

Some hours later, they alighted upon a promising-looking loch that seemed to go on for miles and miles and, as their ancient rattletrap was definitely running much rougher, they decided a rest would do both it and themselves a lot of good. So they called a halt.

They found a suitable piece of flat ground, carpeted with sheep-cropped grass, just half-a mile up a side road and pronounced it ideal for a few days' stay, both loch and village pub being within easy walking distance.

The next midday they adjourned on empty stomachs to the hostelry in question, where they imbibed great swills of ale and, giving vent to raucous peals of laughter and some of the bawdiest of jokes, were at first asked, then ushered, then thrown out by an irate landlord who saw that his tourist trade would diminish rapidly if he did not take things in hand. But not before they had requested, and got, two bottles of whisky and a few crates of that extra-strong Scottish beer which takes so many English visitors by surprise, it being quite a different brew from that which is tendered by their own ale-houses...

Fred and Horace and "Porky", having somehow or other negotiated their way back to their caravan, stumbled into it and, as they clumsily prepared their tackle, swallowed the occasional generous swig of the crater, swilling it down, as they had seen the natives do, with bottle after bottle of the dark, potent stuff which, they reckoned, was the best they had ever tasted. They had already decided that Scotland was a grand place in which to be.

So it was a swaying trio which picked up the necessary gear and headed, around four o'clock, for the "lock". Seeing everything through beer-tinted spectacles, they felt this would be a great day. Skilled as they were in their tactics to tempt big pike even in those waters where the wily brutes had become extra-wary of the fishing fraternity and of all the dupery it concocted to lure them to an untimely death, they were convinced that in this great expanse of water the fish would be both bigger and greener, it being already obvious to them that few, if any, of the local anglers were interested in pike. In fact, they seemed to abhor them, dismissing them as filthy aquatic pigs which should be exterminated, like all vermin. Well, there's no accounting for tastes and they would let them stew in their own pathetic ignorance.

The light boat was pushed out and the staggering, hiccupping, now quite inarticulate three fell into it. It was just as well it was equipped with a small outboard, which fumbling hands finally managed to start, for they could never have held on to oars, let alone used them.

Once a fair distance from the shore and heading towards the almost vertical cliffs on the far side, they duly baited their massive two-inch hooks, all fashioned from the strongest steel by a blacksmith of their acquaintance and sharpened to a needle point, with a variety of offerings. Fred strung on a dozen colossal dew worms, a sight which would have made any game fish unfortunate enough to glimpse them, irrespective of its proportions, set off at unheard-of speed towards the far end of the great waterway. Horace had unqualified faith in the powers of smell and attached to his iron a couple of over-ripe herring heads, while "Porky" preferred a hunk of repulsive-looking maggot-ridden offal tied into a rough ball with a length of red nylon string, a thoroughly jaundiced sausage being added by way of trimming.

These monstrosities were lowered into the depths and enormous chunks of lead, such as one normally associates with sea fishing, were used to force them down. Hazy as they were, the stalwarts from Lancashire noted that even with their outsize spools half-emptied, their weights had not touched the bottom. Little did they know that at that very part of the loch their reels could have emptied many times over and the shingle, mud, rocks - or whatever it was that lay beneath - never reached.

The offal-tosser was soon dozing fitfully and not surprisingly, because, alcoholic intake apart, few humans could have withstood the combination of all the obnoxious odours exuded by the various baits in various stages of freshness - or decay - which were lying in the bottom of the boat. His head hung almost over the side, yet that jumbo rod was still gripped as if held in a vice, and Horace, worried that his friend might go overboard and that their expedition would be curtailed, stabbed his gum-booted foot hard into the tiers of flesh in "Porky's" middle in an effort to arouse him, but to no avail. His only reaction was a deep, wheezy grunt that seemed to come right from the soles of his boots.

However, he did rejoin the realm of the living only minutes later when his rod, his most treasured possession and which he had continued to clutch to his ample gut despite the blow he had received there, was all but wrenched from his grasp. Indeed, had the reel not jammed on the side of the boat, the 15 ft. of solid fibre glass would have sunk out of sight, doubtless forever, into those dark, forbidding depths.

But the barrel-shaped "Porky" was not too stupefied to realise that this might well be the size of beast he had been looking for all his fishing life, a beast which easily surpassed the leviathan he had taken from a local reservoir and which had denied him the British record by a mere six ounces.

He bent his great cleek of a hook and his string-thick nylon and his flagpole of a rod into it to check its downward rush, but without success, and with his hands still glued to the butt he went over to starboard, head-first. He reappeared to port, having been hauled right under the boat, and willing if somewhat groping hands grabbed him and somehow hauled and heaved so that he was at least able to grasp the stern of the rather flimsy craft. Fred and

Tales of Fishing and Fishermen

Horace were quite incapable of pulling him aboard and no doubt just as well, because such an attempt on their part would merely have increased even sooner the precariousness of their situation. But Horace, sweating and cursing, did finally managed to prize the rod from "Porky's" grasp. The latter had still clung to it as if nothing else in the world mattered.

Then, quite slowly, almost majestically, a great head came out of the water and a great tail thrashed the surface. Seconds later the line jumped off the spool, the reel jammed and the light fibre glass boat began to skim over those dark ripples at a speed few racing craft could have matched, with "Porky" still hanging on to it as he lay horizontal to the surface, on his back, with his feet splaying water high into the air.

Very soon a curious crowd, none of whom had, however, arrived in time to catch a glimpse of the brute that had been hooked, had gathered on the shore to enjoy this unrehearsed spectacular. One self-styled wit remarked that aircraft fuel must have been put in the tank by mistake. Others thought it must be water-skiers who had come unstuck, while some just refused to believe their eyes.

Then the giant which had perpetrated these goings-on, aware that it was on a collision course with the tall trees lining the shore, decided to do a quick about-turn without showing any regard whatsoever for the disconcerted souls it was trailing in its wake. The two still aboard soared skywards, followed by their sodden friend - one perspicacious onlooker now shouting that it was definitely practice for a circus act - and three bodies collided in mid-air and fell as one. The boat reared up on its end and disappeared.

Some of the bewildered bystanders had by now realised that help might be required and a conveniently moored motor boat was manned and set in motion and a crazed, bedraggled and dripping trio was hauled aboard, spitting and choking, their eyeballs only just staying in their sockets, and wearing expressions which suggested they might have been to Hell and back.

When one of them had recovered sufficiently to mumble where they had their caravan, they were helped into a car and driven to the site, but on being questioned by the now curiouser-than-ever witnesses as to what on earth had been going on, they responded with one of their uncomprehending stares, from which their interrogators concluded that they should be left alone to recover from their ordeal, whatever it was and whatever had caused it. They could always get the truth out of them the next day.

Once their rescuers had gone, Fred and Horace and "Porky", exhausted, confused and not a little dejected, collapsed on to their beds and succumbed to deep, revitalising sleep.

The next morning the normally unperturbable "Porky" reported that he had had a nightmare, which he went on to describe in detail. The other two could not believe his words, or each others', because they, too, had seen and experienced exactly the same things and it puzzled them that they should all three have had the same bad dream. They didn't think such things could happen, but put it down to the heavy ale and the fact they had mixed it with the golden elixir of the glens.

But having no wish to go through all that again, they hurriedly packed up and pushed off, impatient to head back south, towards kinder drink and sanity.

They got on to the main road and noticed a steamer ploughing through the loch, on its way from Fort William to Inverness.

A Night to Remember

THE DOONIEBURNIE ANGLING CLUB controlled one mile of the main river as well as the entire length of its tributary, the Pauchle and, starved of gregarious opportunity as the villagers were in their remote outpost in the hills, each and every one of them looked forward eagerly to the Annual Social Evening held on the last Saturday of October in the great barn of a hall where, legend had it, their ancestors used to assemble before sallying forth on one of their frequent raids to capture neighbours' cattle and anything else they could lay their hands on. The function took the form of a supper, followed by an address by the secretary and presentation of prizes for the angling competition which had been held in August. Then came a dance. At least that was the official and intended procedure.

The highly-refined dishes which were proffered, normally consisting of pease brose, haggis and neeps and stewed rhubarb and custard, contrasted strangely with the magnificent malts which were always available (malts which had never seen the inside of a distillery, not an official one at any rate) and taken as a whole, the meal would have evoked in any gourmet present alternate bouts of rapture and despair. But then, it must be admitted that fare of even low culinary worth can taste tolerably good if the palate has already been primed with the smooth, golden elixir of the glens. And the Doonieburnians always made sure they had generously imbibed before setting out to partake of a menu that would have made a starving pig think twice, or thrice, before committing itself.

Secretary Seamus Murdoch, seeing that some of those present were already showing unmistakable signs of being blissfully forgetful of their hard daily existence, thought he had better get down to business, although the sumptuous sweet course had not yet been placed before the diners. He stood up, grasping the edge of the table for support:

"Ladies an' geentilmen," he began, "on behalf o' oor Committee - man they dae a grand job, especially me - A huv' tae welcome ye tae this the twenty-second Annual Social Evenin' o' the Doonieburnie Angling Club. A lot o' dirty water has went doon the sink since..."

"Awa', wha ye kiddin'?" bellowed roadman Sanny Naithsmith, "ye huvnae washed yersel' since that nicht ye fell in the Pauchle, an' that wiz aboot three years ago."

"If A may be permitted tae continue wi' ma speech..." went on Seamus.

"Aw, sit doon an' shut that jawbox o' yours, Seamy," intervened a small, rotund figure from the rear of the hall. "Can somebody no' stick a tumbler in his haun' an' then we micht git some peace?"

"Aye, or a blanket ower his heid," bawled Jockie Broon.

"A blanket widnae be near big enough," retorted Sanny, who was in sparkling form, "but there's a tarpaulin lyin' oot there in the yaird."

But Seamus was not to be so easily dissuaded from grasping an opportunity to address and impress an audience, each and everyone of whom he considered to be well below his own intellectual level and quite incapable of his own subtle brand of repertoire. Sweeping a good half-ounce of turnip from the corner of his mouth with the back of his hand on to the ample bosom of the lady sitting next to him, who was none other than big Teenie McTavish, almost circular in shape and all of 18 stones when bone dry (which wasn't often), and renowned far and wide for her elegant carriage and refined oral expression, he soon found himself wishing he had followed his wife's instructions, which were to set an example in etiquette by not taking large mouthfuls of food:

"Look at ma new frock, ya dirty rotten pig, ye. Ye're no in yer sookery noo, ye ken," she yelled at the pitch of her voice, then added as an afterthought on looking about her: "Mind ye, ye should feel quite at hame in this place. Here's it back, wi' interest!"

And, snatching a full fistful of turnip from her neighbour's plate, Teenie plastered it right over Seamus' right and only good eye. Then, just to rub it in, literally, she placed her massive, chubby paw on top of his square, bald pate and pressed down hard, using all of the two hundredweight plus at her disposal. Seamus hit his chair with such a wallop that his every nerve jangled right to the tip of his big toe and beyond. It reminded him of the time he had inadvertently grasped the spark-plug of his old motorcycle while the engine was running.

"Aye, sit doon an' get oan wi' yer neeps. Noo ye'll ken whit thae puir pigs o' yours has tae pit up wi' every day," roared Teenie in a voice like thunder.

Once the dizziness had gone and he had stopped breathing like a pair of clapped-out bellows, Seamus hurriedly swallowed a massive gulp of choice Darlin' Doonie, which was reputed to be about 150% proof, and got to his feet once more, just when the plates of rhubarb and jugs of custard were being banged on to the tables by the waiters hired for the auspicious occasion.

"Sorry aboot the interructions, folks," he said, as heartily as ever, "but ye just huv' tae take the rough wi' the smooth."

"Aye, ye can say that fur this denner," wheezed wee Davy Craw, the brose hud too much tattie peel in it an' that haggis must a' been deid fur aboot a year! If it wiznae fur the whusky ma hert wid a' stopped an' A wid be laid oot oan the flair."

"Ye'll be laid oot oan the flair a' richt if ye guzzle doon oany mair o' that bothy brew," ranted his spouse Maggie as she gave him a look which would have stopped a raging stag in its tracks, "ye've already coughed oot yer false

Tales of Fishing and Fishermen

teeth intae that custard jug withoot kennin' oanything aboot it. A saw them when Stoorie Tam across there wiz pourin' custard oan tae his rhubarb. Ye'll huv' tae gaun roond a' the plates tae see wha's got them."

"Order please! Order!" beseeched Seamus, "A noo come tae the presentation o' the prizes. Noo folks, oor funds has not been too big, an' ye canna mak' a fancy purse oot o' a soo's lug, but just the same, A think ye'll a' agree that we huv' done ye quite magnificent. The first prize fur the heaviest fush gauns tae Roddie McIver fur the salmon he got in February - 21 pund. Whit a beast it wiz! Congratul....."

"It wiz a late spawner o' a kelt!" roared Wee Wullie Huntly, who had taken one of 20 lb. (with a snare) and was annoyed he had been pipped at the post. "A seen it wi' ma ain een. Its belly wiz as flat as Slugger Thompson's nose an' ye wid a' thocht a' the rats in the coup had been at its tail. It's gills were crawlin' wi' maggots the size o' docken grubs an' it hud only yin ee."

"A don't think ye've even got that!" screamed Roddie, whose deepest emotions had been roused. "It wiz a braw fush straight frae the sea."

"Aye, the Redd Sea, haw, haw!" retorted Wullie.

Although even the females present knew that salmon in spawning livery were most unattractive-looking creatures, as different in appearance from fish just arrived from the sea as to make it difficult to believe that they belonged to the same species, and that the hollows they scooped out of the gravel and in which they deposited their eggs were known as "redds", the pun was unfortunately lost on them and most of the males as well as they possessed but scant knowledge of the great, wide world outside their own little glen. Also, it was many years since they had departed from the benches of the local school but Wee Wullie had sweltered in the heat of Aden during the Second World War, so it was a place-name with which he at least had been familiar during his adult life.

Roddie's face had taken on an ominous shade of purple. "Listen tae me, ya stupit wee goat! Thae maggots ye mention were sea lice an' it wiz yin o' thae damned seals that had bitten a wee bit oot o' its tail. Ye're just fu' o' envy, man, that A've got the prize an' you huvnae."

"A wee bit oot o' its tail? A've seen a burn troot wi' a bigger rudder than that!" retaliated Wullie.

"Geentilmen, please, geentilmen!" implored Seamus, "let us no' quarrel oan such a happy evenin'. If Mr. McIver will please tae step forward, ma dear wife here will present him wi' his prize o' a spinnin 'rod.'"

The petite Mrs. Murdoch experienced more than a little difficulty in lifting up the two-piece contraption to hand it to Roddie. When the latter saw it, he surveyed it with dismay and, his face flushed more than ever, he turned on Seamus:

"Wha the hell picked this? It'll be me that'll spin roond if A try tae cast wi' this thing. Whit did ye dae, tie some curtain rings oan a cudgel that could brain an elephant? A'm supposed to tempt the fish wi' a minnin, no' clatter them oan the heid wi' a caber."

"Well, whit are ye complainin' aboot, that's hoo ye fish oanyway, isn't it?" Seamus roared back. He was now becoming a little impatient at the lack of consideration shown for all the trouble he took in his running of the club.

"Awe, shut yer goblet!" counterblasted Roddie, "oanyway, A'm short o' twa strong palin' stabs fur a job A'm daein' in the gairden so A suppose thae twa big thick sticks that ye ca' a fishin' rod'll come in handy fur that. They'll see me oot."

"Aye, fur ye're rotten through an' through already, ye ungrateful skunk, ye!"

But a reproachful nudge from his genteel better-half served to remind Seamus of his elevated position at the gathering and, regaining his former aplomb and dignified bearing, he went on:

"Noo fur the next prize. It gauns tae - A mean goes tae - Bert McCann fur the heaviest broon troot caught oan the flee. A magnificent specimen o' $2^3/_4$ pund, which, A believe, fell tae a wee Black Spider."

"Ye mean it fell tae a big blackheided worm!"

This rather disparaging and quite uncalled-for remark was aimed directly at the recipient of the prize, lofty gardener "Hand-me-down-the Moon" McCann - reputedly the only man in the district who could whitewash his living-room ceiling without using a step-ladder. It was uttered by Danny Stook who felt rather piqued as he had landed a brownie of $2^1/_2$ lb. one evening about a week before the competition and kept it in a deep-freeze at the "Big Hoose", thanks to the kind co-operation of one of the kitchen staff.

"It wiz nae worm. It wiz caught wi' a Spider," came the angry reply.

"Awa', the only spiders that you see are the yins that crawl up an doon the wa' when ye're lyin' in yer bed in the efternin. A saw ye pittin' the worm oan an' throwin' it in!"

"If ye thocht that wiz a worm it's time ye went tae see an optic-, an opticician. An' you're a fine yin tae talk. A suppose that wee red ba' A saw ye pittin' oan yer hook wiz yin o' thae cherries ye stole off Granny Mercer's tree?"

"Noo, noo, chaps, nae mair o' that again - if Mr. McCann will please tae come up here fur tae receive his prize?"

"Keep yer heid doon, Canny," guffawed carpenter Shugh Tarff. "Thae rafters is bein' held up wi' the cobwebs an' we dinnae want the roof tae come doon oan top o' us. It's rainin' ootside."

McCann, all 6 ft. $7^1/_2$ in. of him, contemptuously dismissed this remark with an unmistakable and not very polite sign from two of his lengthy fingers and stepped forward to be handed a waterproof fishing-coat. He unfolded it in full view of the audience:

"Wha's this fur, ma bairn? He's only twa years auld, ye ken, he'll no' be fishin' fur a month or twa yet."

"Never mind, Canny, ye can aye wear it instead o' a bunnet. It's time ye hud a new yin oanyway," tittered old Billy Howker who, over the span of some 60 years, had got through a few "bunnets" himself – two to be exact. "An' ye can pit yer lugs through the sleeves instead o' yer airms."

"And noo," continued Seamus when the uproar had died down, "we come tae the last o' the prizes, last but not least, geentilmen an' ladies, because this is a special prize fur who the Committee huv' judged in their infinitive wisdom tae be the most sportin' fisher amangst us during the past season. Step forward proodly, Henny McNab!"

The diminutive and grisly-faced Henny blushed profusely on hearing that he was the winner of what had always been a cherished award, the ultimate accolade for the love of the gentle art for its own sake and for sheer lack of selfishness on a river that often had more anglers on its banks than fish in its waters. But he tried his best to overcome an overwhelming feeling of guilt and embarrassment and marched up to the table, hands already outstretched.

"Whit, that wee bow-legged hedgehug?" screeched Dunky Todd, his countenance displaying rank disbelief, "he's as twisted as a ba' o' twine the cat's hud! Ye're gi'en him the prize because he gets ye free dung frae his brither's ferm!"

"Noo, noo, Dunky, that kind o' remark is no' very nice, no' very nice at a'. Ye ken fine that A pay fifty pence fur a ton an' a hauf."

Henny's reward for his alleged exemplary display of riverside sportsmanship was a rather slim and unfunctional-looking priest.

"Hey, whit's this? The handle off yin end o' a bairn's skippin' rope? Ye couldnae mak' a dent in a rotten balloon wi' this thing. Hivens, man, huv' ye no' seen the sledge-hammer heid A cairry aboot wi' me?"

"Awa', wha ye kiddin', Henny?" challenged Sam McKendrick, who usually used the steel toe cap of his size 12 boot to dispatch any fish he happened to catch, "that thing they've gi'en ye is heavy enough tae kill oanything ye get a haud o'. It'll be grand fur quarter-pund troots."

It was at this juncture that Seamus received yet another poke from his ever-observant wife and a whispered suggestion (she was a little more knowledgeable in matters of etiquette than he was, but not much) that at future socials the prizes should be wrapped in paper, adding the life-saving clause that if no brown paper was available then newspaper would do. This would also, she maintained, enhance the entire prize-giving ceremony by

A Night to Remember

creating an air of mystery and anticipation. Seamus, now well soaked with Darlin' Doonie and Perky Pauchle, nodded a sort of uncomprehending assent and, relieved that the presentation was over with no untoward verbal and a complete absence of physical scuffles, which was somewhat unusual, slurred out:

"An' noo, folks, the Doonieburnie Quarryblasters is ready fur tae entertain us wi' thur ain special brand o' soft, soothin' music, so A'll ask ye tae get oan tae the flair an' dance tae the first tune, which is a foxfoot - A mean a foxtrot - an' ane o' oor auld favourites - *Strollin' doon the Doonie, far frae the dirty toonie.* The band wull then break into anither foxf..., foxtrot, anither yin that we a' like - *Poachin' doon the Pauchle, when the bailie's oan the bottle.* Noo, folks, get thae flair-boards rattlin'."

Tottering legs did their level best to execute one or two dance steps which might have been most kindly described as being a little short of Fred Astaire standard. Head-on and back-on collisions were frequent but such mishaps were largely ignored by the parties involved, simply because by this time everyone was well anaesthetised against the blows and the thumps and the kicks. Then Sammy Sinclair, (who just made 5 ft. when shod in his home-made clogs), obviously in Casanova mood, managed, by dint of a colossal effort - which entailed standing on tip-toe (not easy with this type of foot-wear) - to get an over-amorous arm round his partner's brawny neck. But Big Teenie was still sore about her neep-stained frock and was in no frame of mind for any hanky-panky, so that Sammy's arm was returned to his side with a twist and a whack like that suffered by many a fish when he drove home his No. 6 hook. But Teenie was only getting steam up:

"So ye want a squeeze, dae ye, ya wee baldy-heided bachle? Well, here's a squeeze ye'll no' forget fur mony a day!"

And, putting both forearms round his neck and clasping her massive hands behind his head, she applied pressure such as could have been exerted only by something like a car-crushing vice. As wee Sammy's face turned red, then purple, then showed ominous signs of black, Teenie eased off with the result that his pipe-worn and tobacco-stained National Health dentures which, under the initial compression, had hit the roof of his mouth, now shot out into the open and ricocheted across the floor. Teenie then lifted her protagonist 2 ft. into the air and, as a farewell gesture, sent him scurrying into a couple absorbed in their own version of a melody called the *Doonieburnie Dandies.* That rather upset their rhythm but even so, Sammy was looked upon as a merely temporary interference and was promptly redirected by the male half of the partnership towards the benches lining the wall. His body-slide was eventually halted when he walloped into the brawny legs of scavenger Lochie Laidlaw who, lulled by his intake of the best

Tales of Fishing and Fishermen

part of a bottle, was just slipping off into oblivion. But the imperturbable Lochie (he didn't even open an eye) simply used one huge tackety boot to sweep Sammy under the bench like so much unwanted garbage. Subjected as he had been to so many trials and tribulations, all in the space of a few seconds, poor Sammy collapsed thankfully against the wall, where he remained, blissfully unaware of his whereabouts, until he was scooped up by two friends and half-carried home a few hours later.

Further turmoil erupted when another would-be Romeo, Trabbie Tulloch by name, had manoeuvred his partner, fiery wee man-hater Lizzie Glen, into a darkish corner and proceeded to plant on her cheek what was supposed to be a tender and inviting kiss. But, not helped by the fact that his great drain of a mouth still bore more than a vestige of greasy haggis and cold custard, Trabbie's well-meaning advances were repelled in no uncertain fashion by a female viper who looked on all men as sexually-motivated animals to be avoided at all costs:

"Dinnae try tae get a' sooky-dooky wi' me, ya dirty auld boar!" she screamed.

At the same time, she raised one bony knee and with all the strength derived from her aversion to the male sex in general and to Trabbie Tulloch in particular, she planted it surely and with telling effect in a place that made Trabbie roar out in agony and run, clutching himself, for the door. Rumour has it that he was never quite the same man thereafter and had to get rid of his breast waders as he could no longer stand in the water above a certain very delicate spot; and that Lizzie gloated for weeks over the fact that she had put out of copulative action, for a spell at least, a member of the detested male sex.

It was just as well, perhaps, that the event took place only once a year, for many of the Doonieburnians came out of it wearied and battle-scarred. But within a few weeks, Seamus was planning a more ambitious evening for the following October, one which, he hoped, would be held in the magnificent new motel just being completed at the head of the glen. French waiters, exotic menus, candle-lit tables, everything very much *à la posh*.

The goings-on will be reported in full in due course.

Tongue an' Cheek

THE ESTATE FACTOR raised his binoculars and at first thought either they or his eyes were playing him tricks.

"Yes, by God, you're right, Robby! They *are* fishing. Must be real idiots, in open country like this. Damn' cheek! Let's go!"

Factor and head keeper got back into their Range Rover and headed upstream towards a point which provided the shortest route to the two infidels who had the audacity to ply their rods on one of the most sanctified and peerless salmon streams of the far North-West. Indeed, it was maintained locally that it would be easier for the Devil to acquire a ticket guaranteeing him entrance through the Gates of Heaven than for any ordinary citizen to gain legitimate access to these hallowed pools.

Factor and keeper leapt from their vehicle and stamped through the heather, surprised and not a little annoyed that the two intruders had not taken to their heels.

"May I ask what you think you are doing?"

"What are we doing?"

The French accent - or at least the foreign accent - was very marked. "Fishing, sir!"

The Factor almost exploded. He hadn't dealt with this type before. He fumed from a face that had turned a dangerous purple:

"No fishing here."

"No fish in here? But yes, we see fish jump all the time. Lovely big salmons. Look, there is one now. At least six kilos!"

The purple deepened even further.

"You can NOT fish HERE."

"Yes, we can fish. We have rods and these hooks and - what you call them? - vorms?"

"Holy mackerel!" gasped the keeper. But he noticed only a shred of rather dilapidated worm clinging precariously to a No. 6 hook. He didn't know that the writhing mass of four or five large blackheads had been hastily torn off at the first sign of their approach.

The Factor said no more for the moment, but only because speech was, for him, a physical impossibility. Only his face revealed his thoughts, thoughts which were as black and ominous as the storm-clouds now scudding up the sea loch from the Atlantic. "Bloody stupid foreigners" was complimentary compared with most of the others. A pragmatist who was apt to condemn too many fields of knowledge as being purely academic and of little practical value, he admitted to himself, for the first time in his life, that the ability to converse in tongues other than one's own might sometimes be useful.

Another salmon threw itself into the air.

"A big one, *n'est-ce pas?* I try to catch him now, with leetle vorm!"

The keeper thought his Factor was about to run off berserk into the heather, but the latter finally managed to splutter:

"Oh, for God's sake, Robby, come on!"

Each grabbed one of the wrong doers by an arm and they were marched off. They objected strongly, their most vehement protests being expressed in very rapid French. They were pushed right to the road, right to their parked Dormobile.

"Now go away and do **NOT** come back! Next time it's the **POLICE**."

Their faces revealing incomprehension and even bewilderment, the two malefactors drove off. Factor and keeper watched them until their vehicle disappeared from view.

"Granted that they are just plitterers and have no chance of taking a fish, but a lot of these Continentals are now coming up here on holiday and they're a damn' nuisance to say the least. Better patrol a bit more, Robby. Get McIntyre to help you."

The departed Dormobile headed downstream for Scourie and the South. During the days that followed, it made further stops at other delectable streams which, if they did not quite aspire to the incomparable standard of the one where they had had their latest fracas, were not too far behind.

Some time later, the same vehicle came to a halt outside a fishmonger's in Glasgow and from it's Calor-gas freezer nearly 50 salmon were extracted. A large sum of money changed hands.

"Three or four times wasn't it, we were put off, Colin?" said the taller of the two language students. "Great fun, great profit, eh? But better we give that area a rest for a spell. What about Spey and Dee next week?"

A Man and his Otter

DONALD McINTYRE, perhaps the epitome of the giant Highland bobbie who had come to town, had retired from the Metropolitan Police and the bustling hive that was London, to return home to his corner of Inverness-shire and search out a quiet nook where he could live the totally unsophisticated life he preferred, far from the superficialities and make-believe and bogus values of what was reputed to be a high level of civilisation.

He had bought himself a solidly built cottage and to achieve the two-fold purpose of eking out his pension and improving his property, had taken a job as general handyman on the local estate. At weekends he would regularly tramp off into the hills with his binoculars and his fishing rod and spend a few hours by a little-visited loch, with only the hawks, the buzzards and the deer for company. And the occasional eagle.

Then had come the day when, walking by the great salmon river during an otter-hunt, he had been attacked by one of the estate hounds, a larger than normal specimen with a peculiar dark patch behind one ear. It had bitten him in the leg, and for its trouble, had received some thumping blows from the stout stick he always carried.

His act of retaliation (but not the dog's act of aggression) had been noted by the Master of Hounds and since animals, even dangerous ones, are sometimes placed on a loftier rung in the social hierarchy than human beings, Don had been allowed no further than the estate gate on reporting for work the following morning. His leg had troubled him periodically ever since and he swore that if the chance of revenge ever presented itself, he would seize it with both hands.

Ironically, Don was a great animal-lover, provided the beast was gentle and sensible or only acting in accordance with the natural role it had been given. But he had little time for unprovoked viciousness in any shape or form, whether the culprit was man or beast.

Following his sacking, Don had completed various gardening projects for big houses in the area, laying paths and rockeries and constructing the odd fish-pond. He was master of his own day and the nature of his employment left him many free hours for walking by the river. It was during one of those forays that he found Sadie.

The otter-hounds had been out and had torn her mother, father and her two brothers to pieces. Sadie, being the smallest of the pups, had wormed her way through a tiny hole at the rear of the holt and penetrated what was to the dogs an inaccessible part of the bank, thus being spared a similar fate. She had emerged some time later, and, scared and bewildered and calling plaintively, she had wandered down to the water's edge.

Don had picked her up in his great shovel-like hands and cradled her in his arms and in some mysterious manner an instant bond had been fashioned

Tales of Fishing and Fishermen

between a man who loved animals and an animal which knew nothing of man, not even that it was he who, for mere enjoyment, had robbed her of kith and kin.

Sadie had quietened down and Don had taken her home and forced milk down her throat. The following day, she had drunk it without compulsion.

The insurmountable barrier of instinctive distrust that so often exists in the mind of a wild creature, even a young one, when confronted with a human being, gradually evaporated and in a matter of a few weeks, Sadie had become quite relaxed in her master's presence and had begun to follow him around the garden.

Don had fed her with eels from the burn which skirted his property and there too he had dug out a broad, deep pool so that Sadie could make her own catches and dive and swim and frisk about as far as the limits of the pool allowed. Occasionally, she would make off upstream, the glint of adventure in her bright little eyes, but she always returned on hearing Don's strident whistle.

She always returned because deep and mutual ties of friendship had been formed between a growing otter, which should have known naught but water, pine and bracken, and a huge ex-policeman, who had seen life in both its shabbiest and most sophisticated forms and knew what was worthwhile and what was not.

When Sadie was well on the way to being a mature bitch otter, Don knew he had to face up to the problem that had been haunting him for some time. He knew it was no longer fair to keep penned up in a garden and its adjacent burn a creature whose birthright was the untrammelled freedom of the element that was her natural habitat.

And so, one fine autumn morning, when Sadie was a year and a few months old, he took her back, albeit with a heavy heart, to the broad salmon river by whose rocky sides she had been born. For some time, Don watched her as she performed her usual aquabatics, tumbling and rolling and diving joyfully, her powerful shoulders bursting with strength and vitality.

This was where she belonged, not to a small burn with an extended pool and a dog-kennel for a holt. Then, convinced that if he did not act now it would amount to nothing less than a flagrant contradiction of all he stood for, he took a last lingering look. Then he turned and fled.

Later that evening, while he sat lonely and pensive in his front room, a raucous whimpering drew him from his armchair.

Sadie had come home. She stood on the back doorstep, looking up at him, a grilse in her mouth.

Their liaison had proved stronger than all the wild, magnetic callings of Nature. And Don was happy. He had offered Sadie her freedom but she preferred to stay with him. He could now let his mind rest.

Man and otter often went back to the broad salmon river, where one mused and the other played. And many fine salmon and sea trout came home with them.

The only threat to this idyllic existence was the periodic otter-hunt, but Don kept Sadie well away from the river on such days, of which he was always informed in advance by Tom Purdie, an old friend who acted as grieve on the estate.

Then came a mild autumn morning with veils of steel blue mist clinging to the steep sides of the glens. Don whistled for Sadie and off he went with her beside him, not knowing that Tom Purdie had been sent away for several days to help out on an estate near Fort William.

They reached the river and Don walked quietly along the bank, noticing the great clumps of heather that were now at their Highland best, while Sadie dived into the peaty depths and proceeded to make the pool boil with her antics.

After half-an-hour the sun shone hot and Don sat down on the short grass which matted the bank. Sadie came and lay beside him for a few minutes, and then, full of the restlessness and the vitality of youth, returned to her water games.

Don's thoughts began to wander. Lost in reverie, his eyelids closed and he succumbed to sleep.

He awoke with a start to the sound of loud, sustained yapping. Sadie! Alarmed, he jumped to his feet. At the same moment, about 100 yds. downstream, a devilish uproar developed at the foot of a pine whose roots had been eroded. He rushed headlong towards the spot.

Sadie had been dragged from her hiding place and was surrounded by at least half-a-dozen dogs.

As Don reached the scene, she was being mauled in merciless fashion by a large hound with a conspicuous patch behind one ear. It was literally tearing her apart.

The dark, powerful forces that often lurk behind an outwardly even temperament flooded to the surface. Don rushed forward and as he grabbed the hound by the loose skin behind its neck, it transferred its viciousness from otter to man, trying to sink its teeth into his thigh. He kicked it in the belly with all the force of his hobnailed boot, then he pulled it to him and encircled its throat with those massive hands. And he squeezed the breath out of it. The other hounds scurried off.

Once more he picked Sadie up and cradled her, just as he had done the day they first met, and while the life-blood from her broken body drained away on his arms, she looked out of misty eyes into his and managed a hoarse little squeak as he hugged her gently.

Then she quivered and was gone.

Inconclusive?

JOHNNIE SIMS had accrued as many notches on his rod butt as any other permit-holder on the five miles of association water, and more than most. Besides being a three or four times a week visitor to the river, which, as everyone knows, is what counts for overall success in catching temperamental salmon, he was methodical, persistent and highly skilled, whether it was with fly, minnow, worm, or whatever. If Johnnie Sims was not catching fish, there was little hope for anyone else.

Sims had had his share of larger than average specimens and it was the months of September, October and November which he liked best, that being the period when his Solway river produced its big "back-enders", often as fresh and as beautiful as the most delectable springers from Dee or Tay, great husky brutes which for sheer strength and tenacity, were and still are, unequalled anywhere. Over the years he had grassed a dozen of them topping 30 lbs, with the largest scaling just over 35. But he knew they ran much heavier, and in fact on three occasions had lost goliaths when his line had broken or his hooks had straightened. And, commendable as his record was, he still longed to land a salmon which was in a class of its own, one which would turn the scales to an unprecedented figure and make every beholder stare in awe at the reading. This was his great ambition and he would almost have sold his casting-arm to the Devil in order to attain it. Irrational but true.

On that fifteenth day of October the morning was mild with a steady breeze and Johnnie Sims was on the bank by the time it was fully light. Having fruitlessly worked a No. 6 Black Doctor through a long, rough stream called The Sluice, obviously well-tenanted with new arrivals, he exchanged fly rod for spinner and attached a 3-inch brown and gold, the points of its new treble honed to needle-sharpness.

A third of the way down the stream he got the expected stop and soon had a bright nine-pounder in his net. Having retied both minnow and swivel, he recommenced operations.

He had almost reached the tail when the line tightened. Stuck solid. He cursed, anticipating the loss of a splendid new minnow fashioned by his own hand. He walked as far as he could upstream to vary the angle but the hooks refused to budge. Then back downstream, hoping the drag of the extra line pulled from his reel would jerk the minnow free. But no, it was impaled as firmly as ever. He laid down his rod to go and fetch his otter from his creel and on picking it up again, he was certain that the angle of the line, when taut, was at least 20 degrees different. And upstream at that. But by the law of nature, obstructions such as branches or coils of wire or cattle-feed bags don't move against the current, and with bated breath Sims applied the butt until his stout spinning rod was bent double and his 20 lb. line was singing and sighing in the wind. Then, when the pressure became too great, and he dared apply no more, he felt the faintest response. The fish, if that's what it was, moved about an inch.

He eased the pressure, released an explosive breath, refilled his lungs and repeated the process. Another inch.

The third time the fish did not move at all. Nor the fourth. "God!" thought Sims, "what do I do?" He glanced upstream and down. Not a soul to be seen. Not that anyone could have done much to help in any case.

He knew he would be there for ever if he did not rouse the salmon from its lethargy, its apparent unawareness of the circumstances, or from whatever it was that rendered it motionless. If he could not make it move, he would be as well to cut his line and call the whole thing off.

A couple of rocks aimed at the right spot made not the slightest impression on the fish and Sims knew he had to apply all the force of which he and his tackle were capable. If the line broke or the hooks straightened then that would be that. But it was the only way.

He gave it all he had. And it moved what must have been a couple of inches. Sims felt he could have elicited more response from a bag of sand or cement. His arms aching, and gasping continually with the effort, he continued to haul it towards him an inch or two at a time, sometimes less.

This went on, incredibly, for an hour and ten minutes, the fish sometimes slowly and effortlessly moving back a couple of feet, which undid the work of 15 slogging minutes. By this time Sims had reached a state of near exhaustion. This creature did not belong to the usual salmon breed. Even his 35-pounder had started to run after a few rude proddings from the butt, but this leviathan was a law unto itself, apparently with no idea of what it was supposed to do.

But he kept on heaving, gasping and hauling. He had no option for there was no other action he could take. But how long would his tackle stand up to this merciless pounding? Even a 20 lb. line and hand-forged trebles had their limits. As had his muscles and his heart.

One hour forty minutes. Sim's features were now drawn, his arms leaden, his legs weak and shaking. He tottered each time he tried to change his stance.

Then he gained some recuperation, of mind if not of body, from the fact that in spite of his abject weariness he could now pull his antagonist about six inches towards him in a single attempt. Then the six inches became a foot. He realised that the salmon, too, had weakened.

The problem was - who would be first to capitulate?

He finally worked it into the deep eddy at the edge of the pool and its tail

41

came out of the water. If what he saw was an indication of the fish's size, which of course it was, then this was the Atlantic salmon not just of his own lifetime but of anyone's lifetime. It had to be a freak, one of those oddities thrown up by nature now and again just to show that the exception maketh the rule.

He kept up the pressure as far as his own rapidly waning strength allowed.

Two hours and five minutes had elapsed when he finally managed to pull the fish almost to the bank. It was just below the surface in 8 ft. of water and as it turned on its side, what he saw made his heart race even more, which, as he knew, had its dangers. His adversary seemed to be about $1^1/2$ ft. deep and somewhere between 4 and $4^1/2$ ft. long.

His emotions now bordered on a sort of silent hysteria. He was within an ace of landing this monster which, without a shadow of doubt, would put itself in the record books for all time. Would his tackle hold out? Could *he* hold out?

His landing-net, which could take a 30-pounder comfortably, looked hopelessly inadequate for the task in hand and he rejected it. He would try to beach the fish on the only spit of gravel available (thanks to God it was there) and trust he had just enough strength left to get behind it, grab the broad wrist of that Concorde-like tail and slide the salmon out of the water and up on to the grass. He would simply fall on top of it and stay there until it expired.

The giant now lay practically motionless on the surface, completely and utterly exhausted, its gills hardly functioning at all. Sims stepped to one side and his rod and line took the fish's weight once again and for what, he hoped, would be the last time.

2 ft. from the gravel. A matter of seconds.

Then came the most sickening feeling known to an angler, the sudden recoil as the rod springs back as if shot from a catapult. The treble hook which had taken such a battering for two hours and fifteen minutes had finally had enough. The main barb holding the fish had snapped off. At the same time, Sims saw the mammoth salmon, victor at the very last moment, sink down slowly into the depths, out of his reach but by no means out of his life.

Sims collapsed on to the turf and sank his head in his hands. He sat there for a long time and then he went home.

It was in the afternoon of the same day that a couple of young boys arrived breathless at the bailiff's house:

"Mr. Watson, there's a huge fish lying dead at the side of the river. We think it must be a porpoise or a dolphin or something!"

Inconclusive?

The salmon was retrieved and taken to the bailiff's house. The news soon spread and Sims, wondering, went to see it with all the others, who stared unbelievingly. The bailiff said it weighed $68^1/_2$ lbs.

Sims prised its mouth open and on one side saw ragged flesh and congealed blood. He ran his finger over the wound and felt a sharp prick.

But he kept his own mouth shut. The evidence was weighty, all right, but inconclusive.

Bridge over Troutless Waters

THE HALF-MILE of water bequeathed to Angus McNaught at Durlannich, on a tributary of a mighty northern river, had excellent runs of sea trout, but Angus was for ever bemoaning the fact that he could not have had a more unproductive stretch had he been given the choice. Certainly he grassed some smallish fish in daylight when there was extra water, using very small flies and the flimsiest nylon. But in the ultra-dry summers which seemed to have developed into a permanent weather pattern, he had little opportunity even for that, the water being too thin to hold anything but parr and suchlike. And even night fishing was out, the beatlet being so annoyingly shallow that all he could do was watch and listen to the trout, some of them in the 5-6 lb. range, scud and tear their way through it as they desperately sought the sanctuary of deeper and safer waters further upstream, which, of course, were outwith his boundaries and belonged to someone else.

It was when British Rail finally closed the branch line, which cut right across his land and over the river about the middle of his little beat, that an idea occurred to him.

Angus enlisted the help of an old friend, an ex-Army engineer skilled in demolition work, for whom he had done the odd favour himself.

It took some time to acquire the essential materials for, naturally, great caution had to be exercised. No other living soul had to know or even guess what was going on.

Everything was made ready while the river was low. Impatiently, Angus waited for the right moment to down the plunger, and the right moment eventually came - a night with a howling gale. The strength of the old structure had been under official suspicion for some time. And a hurricane also serves to cancel out other sounds...

Thus, deadened by the elements - there was prolonged and drenching rain as well - the detonations were heard by no one apart from the two who effected them. Angus and his colleague departed from the scene, satisfied that things could not have gone better.

He was back at first light.

The bridge had done its job. Ton upon ton of ironwork and masonry were piled on the river bed, forming a compact, almost impenetrable barrier to the downward flow of water. As the river rapidly rose, the newly-formed barrage became firmer as the current drove the various smaller pieces closer together, welding them into a near-solid mass. The stretch above where the bridge had been was now a broad, deepish pool, a pool which would hold fish... Angus smiled contentedly, anticipating great days and nights to come, as he saw sea trout struggle through the channels at both extremities of the dam, where the accumulation of debris was not so concentrated, and beam tantalising into the water above.

As the river quickly dropped back to summer level the previously useless broken stretch above the site of the bridge now boasted a depth of 5 ft. in parts and was obviously holding a good head of trout, especially in the tail. The first night following

the transformation, Angus reeled in eight of them between 10.30 and 1 o'clock and lost as many more.

Each outing was almost a repetition of the one before. Some produced more than others, as they invariably do, and there was even the occasional blank when the temperamental creatures completely spurned his succulent Ghost Swift Moths and his bushy Black Spider, but it was a below average night if his creel weighed less than 8 or 9 lb. In one wonderful week, he netted more fish than he had done in the whole of the previous season.

All this transpired just before the end of the university year, which meant the return home of his son, Donald, a student at St. Andrews, to whom he was very close. He couldn't wait for Donald to arrive - he usually just appeared unexpectedly on the doorstep - because he too was a keen angler and no doubt in need of some restorative relaxation after a particularly trying term. He would have a welcome surprise, having deplored the impoverished state of the stretch almost as much as his father.

When the mainline train to the north finally reached the station, a good five miles from the cottage, Donald got out the old bike which he always left in the stationmaster's shed to facilitate such journeys and to save money on taxi fares. His father had no car, having little need for one, as he rarely strayed from the confines of the glen.

As Donald moved off, he was suddenly conscious of the extreme sultriness of the night and could hear not-too-distant rumblings over towards Durlannich. A cracker of a storm was obviously brewing.

He felt the first drops on his face and, remembering his father had told him in a letter that the branch line was now finally and irrevocably closed, he decided to shorten his route home and reduce the measure of his discomfort by cycling along the track. He reckoned it would cut his journey almost by half.

Eager to gain the paternal roof, he pressed on into the night. Within minutes he was drenched to his very bones and three-quarters blinded by the unremitting downpour. It was all he could do to stay on the narrow cinder track between the still unlifted rails and the grass verge. But, head down, he kept going, determined to get there and be rid of his sodden clothes at the earliest possible moment.

*   *   *

It was Angus who found him early the next morning when he crashed through the ferns to emerge at the water's edge just above the barrage he had created to add to his own and his son's pleasure, impatient to be there to try the worm down the enticing eddies developing at the side of the dam as the flood reached its height.

Donald lay wedged in grotesque fashion across the top of the iron and the masonry, one arm extended upwards towards where the bridge had been, the other pointing straight at his father.

Loophole

THE WORTHY inhabitants of Garriestanes could hardly believe what they saw as they scanned a long article in the *Garriestanes Gabbler*, the journal which served as gossip-sheet for their own Highland airt. Mackie's, a large tackle-making firm of national and even international repute, had found that an ever-increasing demand by an ever-growing army of anglers made it imperative that an additional factory should be set up. They had decided on little-known Garriestanes, where unemployment was high and what employment there was, rough. The project would create at least twenty jobs initially, almost certainly more later as the premises were extended. With the buildings sited on the edge of the moor, space would present no problem. No great skill needed either. Just the will to learn and good old Highland industriousness.

If the majority of the Garriestanians were pleased because such an enterprise promised regular work and work of a nature far removed from the back-breaking, heart-breaking toil of moor and forest and the eternal buffeting by the elements, then the anglers amongst them were delighted. Those addicted to the so-called gentlest of arts could already visualise prospects of procuring new and better tackle at prices more in line with their limited means.

Their enthusiasm was further bolstered by a huge advertisement on another page saying that the firm of Mackie Tackle Limited, in order to show they meant well in the neighbourhood and to establish amicable relations right from the outset, intended to organise periodic competitions on a nearby loch and to offer some of their magnificent products as prizes. The first, in fact, would be held shortly after the factory-building operations had begun, early in September. Full details would be published in an early edition of the *Garriestanes Gabbler*.

More than one Garriestanian let his imagination run riot as he savoured the exciting possibilities and no one was disappointed when, a fortnight before the event was due to take place, the *Gabbler* again displayed a large advertisement which gave all the relevant details:

MACKIE TACKLE LIMITED
GREAT AUTUMN COMPETITION
(No Entry Fee)
SATURDAY, September 12, 7 am - 6 pm, Loch Goonie.
ANY LEGAL METHOD ALLOWED. ANY SPECIES WILL COUNT.
FIRST PRIZE FOR HEAVIEST OVERALL CATCH: Choice of
any MACKIE fly and spinning outfits, both complete
in every detail, down to large comprehensive selection

of flies and minnows, spacious fishing bag, pair of
famous MACKIE "Aqualite" breast waders and large net.
SECOND PRIZE: MACKIE fly outfit and spinning outfit
together with box of flies or minnows.
TEN CONSOLATION PRIZES (in descending order of value):
Breast waders, spinning-reel, thigh waders, fishing-bag,
creel, fly-tying outfit, minnow-making outfit, large
thermos, all-purpose knife.
WEIGH-IN. All participants must report at Murray the
Fishmonger's by 7 pm
MACKIE TACKLE WISHES ALL COMPETITORS THE VERY BEST OF
LUCK

It made Garriestanian eyes boggle, not least the eyes of that eminently
downtrodden pair, "Clunker" Condie and Drookie Doak:
"Hey, Clunker, by Jove, eh? We'll hive tae get in oan this. Whit a chance
tae get some decent tackle!"
"Aye," retorted his comrade in perpetual distress, "ma larch pole's been
crackin' fur a year or twa noo. An' ma auld Malloch screams an' squeals like
a litter o' hungry pigs."
Clunker and Dookie, by no means the most accomplished exponents of the
piscatorial art, ate everything they caught, be it pike, perch, or anything that
swam. And, in fact, so hopelessly philistine were their tastes that they
perceived little difference, gastronomically or aesthetically, between these
coarse, bony and often unbeautiful creatures and the splendid form and
succulent flesh of salmon or trout. Whatever was in their trough, they
gobbled up with the same gusto. That was the whole point of the exercise. It
was rather like a dog gulping down a choice liqueur chocolate - done so fast
and with such avidity that taste is of no consequence, only the pleasure, the
animal satisfaction, of quickly replenishing an empty belly.
Even so, they enjoyed their fishing for its own sake, for it provided a
welcome release from the harsh labours of ditch and peat-bog and if they
were rough and rustic in their approach to all things, they were basically
honest and staunch friends who remained loyal to each other in every
respect. So it was not surprising that, should either of them win one of the
main prizes, they agreed to share it out equally. And so they were standing at
the side of Loch Goonie by starting-time, rods at the ready.
Loch Goonie was one of those long and fairly broad expanses of water,
reed-fringed in the shallow areas, forbidding and sinister in its pitch-black
depths, which held good stocks of both game and coarse fish and perhaps
other things besides, all of which seemed quite happy to share a common

Tales of Fishing and Fishermen

habitat, although it must be admitted that they each favoured certain parts and did not encroach too frequently on alien territory. Both Clunker and Dookie knew intimately where specimens of the various species were likely to be, and decided to go after one of the gigantic pike. With their massive rods and 25 lb. lines, they certainly had the required tackle.

Clunker attached a cast of even heavier breaking strain than his line and to his No. 4 hook, he fixed a couple of rotting herring-heads. Dookie used similar tackle but his choice of bait was a bullfrog, also in a state of semi-decay.

These dainty and dignified offerings were despatched with befitting finesse into the calm waters of Loch Goonie. It was difficult to tell which made the biggest splash, the frog or the herring-heads, or the one inch iron nuts being used for casting-weight.

A good two hours went by without a single twitch from either line. As they could see others in the distance draw out the odd fish - perch and trout - they decided to move further up the loch. Perhaps the spot they had chosen was untenanted that day. There were others they could try.

Still nothing to give the slightest encouragement. They moved again and again. Still nothing. Finally, as 4 o' clock approached, desperation began to show, both on their countenances and in their actions.

"C'moan, Dookie, the Witch's Broom. It's oor last chance."

The Witch's Broom was a large protruding rock near the top end of the loch, where they had triumphed on several previous occasions. The large pike seemed to favour it.

Dookie swung back his rod to make his usual delicately executed forward cast, hoping to land his last remaining frog in the very spot he had chosen, just to the left of the Broom. His aim was good, very good, perhaps just too good, because as the stinking bait dropped waterwards, a hefty swan glided out from behind the rock and, to its surprise and annoyance, the tasty morsel, at least tasty for an indiscriminating pike, landed square on its back. Its feathers rose and it honked and quawked and hissed as it lurched away. The big hook, jerked out of the puddock on impact, slid forwards and gripped it low down in the neck.

"Aw Christ!" roared Dookie, "it's jist no' oor day!"

The swan tried to take off but the heavy line held and the high tension ensured that it could not obtain the necessary speed and lift to become airborne. Eventually, when it was exhausted, Dookie was able to pull it towards him. It came like a toy boat on a string.

While Dookie was thus engaged, Clunker muttered something under his breath and pulled a crumpled piece of paper from his pocket. He glimpsed at it, as if confirming his thoughts, then:

"We're takin' this big bugger tae the weigh-in."

"Eh, whit? A bloody swan? Whit fur? It's fish we're supposed tae catch."

"Mebbe no'. Bit never mind the noo. A'll explain it tae ye in a meenit. When ye bring it tae the side, A'll git this bag ower its heid an' we'll tie its feet thegither an' then A'll tell ye."

Dookie looked completely dumbfounded, but decided there was nothing to be lost by complying. After a momentous struggle, the operation was successfully accomplished and a very perplexed and irate swan was taken prisoner.

"Noo," began Dookie, when he had recovered sufficient breath to enable him to question his friend once more, "d'ye mind explainin' whit guid this is gaun tae dae us? Are we gaun tae ate it?"

"Naw, we're no. Too chuch, even fur us, even if ye boiled it fur a week. Bit listen an' A'll tell ye. Read this advert again!"

"A ken whit's oan it. A've read it already, ye ken!"

"Read it again!"

Dookie did but still stared as uncomprehendingly as ever at his friend.

Clunker went on:

"Whit diz it say? It says: ANY SPECIES WILL COUNT. FIRST PRIZE FOR HEAVIEST OVERALL CATCH."

"Eh?"

"Aw fur Goad's sake, Dookie, dae ye no' see whit A mean? It diznae say nothin' aboot it huvin' tae be a fish! It diznae even say it's a *fishin'* competition."

"A' richt, a' richt, bit so whit?"

"So whit? Weel, we caught this big bugger, didn't we? It's oor overall *catch*."

"Och, A see noo." Then, after a moment's hesitation:

"Bit it'll never work, Clunker. They'll think we've gaun daft."

"We'll show them we're no sae daft. If we dinnae get a big pike, this is gaun tae the weigh-in."

Then he added, on reflection, "Aye, even if we dae get yin, it's still gaun."

Which it did. At first the organisers thought it was a huge joke, but both they and the attendant local journalist appreciated the quaint comic touch which the paper would happily print as an interesting news item. Mackie's too would welcome it as good, unexpected publicity. It was titbits such as these that caught the reader's eye and made them talk. And talk meant sales. They were all for that.

But the same organisers were not long in finding out that the firm of Condie and Doak were in deadly earnest. Dookie was at first possibly a little less so, but he soon warmed to the fray, lending whole-hearted support to his enterprising comrade-in-arms.

Clunker waved the clipping in front of the chief organiser's face: "Ye said

Tales of Fishing and Fishermen

nothin' in yer advert aboot *fish*. Ye said *oany species* an' that the heaviest *catch* wid get the First Prize. Weel, this is ma friend's catch, isn't it? An' it's the heaviest, as far as A can see. Bit get it oan thae scales if ye're no convinced!"

The sharper minds amongst Mackie's representatives hesitated, then entered into a short discussion. One of them, who had some knowledge of the law, rushed off to 'phone the firm's solicitors, who advised them to "proceed with caution". Heads again pressed together, for an immediate decision had to be taken.

They all agreed that the situation offered a heaven-sent opportunity for nationwide publicity, an opportunity to prove what a fair-minded firm Mackie's was - and that it had a sense of humour as well. The public would lap it up and the name Mackie would be on everyone's lips. It would be cheap at the price.

So Dookie received what was called a "Special Prize". In fact it included the same number of items, identical in every way, as received by the winner proper, the captor of a 6 lb. pike and a couple of $1/2$ lb. perch. Strangely enough, his name was Harry Swann.

Dookie's prize of miscellaneous items was, of course, shared as equally as possible with Clunker, each of them getting what he needed most.

And the bird itself, which had a distinctive black patch on top of its head and had needed more than 20 lb. of weights to balance the scales on which it had been precariously placed, was taken, still hissing and squawking and honking, back to the loch and released. But its unique and painful experience had not been entirely in vain. Dookie and Clunker, now affluent in the tackle line, if still destitute in everything else, always throw it a bit of their tack each time they encounter it on the loch.

The Lesson

ONE NIGHT Big Teenie McTavish, tired of living in a village which provided few amenities for its womenfolk and seeing its men forever going off to fish their beloved Doonie or its tributary, the Pauchle, called her equally frustrated cronies together to see what could be done to remedy the situation. The outcome was a strongly-worded petition to the Doonieburnie Angling Club to make fishing tuition available to the *gentler* sex. Yes, gentler sex. Remember the Doonieburnie Social?

The committee, aware that they would have even greater problems if they failed to concur, decided that each lady would be assigned to one of its members who would act as her coach, and that, as the female population of the village had a high proportion of assertive and even potentially dangerous characters in its ranks, it was only fair to the men, who shuddered at the dire prospects involved, that the ladies names went into one hat and their mentors' into another. They were then drawn in pairs. Fair play for all.

Danny Stook emitted something like a death-rattle and almost collapsed in a heap when the secretary announced the first coupling - himself and Big Teenie. The others sighed with undisguised relief, glad that fate had been kind to them in that they had at least escaped the worst ordeal of all.

Teenie wasted no time. She had lived long enough in an anglers' paradise to know that the heavy rain then falling would produce a flood the following day. And that was when trout could most easily be caught on worm. So, as soon as she knew who her teacher was to be, she stamped round to his house to inform him that her first lesson was imminent. It would, in fact, take place the next morning.

"Noo, Teenie, are ye sure ye want tae gaun fishin'?" Danny was still unconvinced that Teenie's vowed intention to take up the sport - and he was aware that she had instigated the whole thing among the women - was not just a trick concealing some ulterior design of which only the "weaker" sex, and she in particular, was capable.

"Of course A'm sure. A want tae fish!"

"But dae ye realise it can often be cauld an' wet an' . . ."

"Ach, stop treatin' me like a frail wee lassie, will ye? A could lift up the lot o' yer fishin' pals, burl them roond ma heid an' throw them awa'."

Danny had no answer to that. He knew it was only too true, that she wielded a garden spade or a hayfork with ease and even with gusto. She had the strength - some, less kind, would have added the features - of a working horse. And, handling worms would certainly not bother her, for she cringed before no living creature, either man or beast. He wondered, however, about dexterity, for he had heard about her antics with normally harmless things

like a feather duster on the few occasions she had been employed in the Big House – and the resultant shattering of glass and china.

But the redoubtable Teenie had already procured herself an old cane rod, a spinning-reel and a few bait casts. Trembling with trepidation but realising full well that even a worse fate might await him if he did'nt turn up, Danny duly presented himself at the Auld Brig at the appointed hour of 9 am.

The Doonie was coming down in raucous, roaring flood, more impatient than ever to get to the not-too-distant Atlantic and spread its waters far and wide, something for which it had little opportunity in the confines of its narrow valley. It was coloured into the bargain, providing ideal conditions for initiating anyone into fishing techniques which did not demand too much by way of finesse.

Teenie, perhaps to show that she was well up to the task in hand and that she was inferior to no man, insisted on attaching the slobbery red worm with her own great chubby fingers. Then Danny showed her how to cast it, releasing the bale-arm and holding the line on the spool with the finger, then lifting the latter while sending the worm upstream so that it would come trundling down through the inviting eddies next to the bank.

But since even the most dexterous amongst the uninitiated require a little practice before the rudiments are mastered, it is perhaps not surprising that Teenie sent the bait slap into the middle of an overhanging branch.

"Wait a meenit," said Danny in a gentle tone, careful not to vent his true feelings. "A think A can get up that tree an' free it. Nae use wastin' a guid hook."

He scaled the tree and, disentangling the cast, threw it downwards. He couldn't have hit the target better if he had tried. The worm, still intact, caught Teenie fair and square across her massive chops. Not that that bothered her unduly - what riled her was her firm belief that Danny had done it intentionally.

"Ye rotten bugger!" she roared, "ye did that on purpose!"

"Naw, A didnae," pleaded Danny, who had felt physical expression of her wrath before and had some idea of what to expect.

He got down from his perch and came running towards her, his face pregnant with a sympathy that was not entirely sincere:

"Aw, A'm sorry, Teenie! Let me wipe yer face, hen. A didnae mean tae dae it . . ."

"Dinnae you *hen* me, ye scraggy auld craw!" And, dropping her rod and picking up Danny's huge net, she planted it firmly over his head and right down over his shoulders. Then, pushing hard on the shaft, she sent her would-be mentor crashing backwards into a dense patch of undergrowth that was a mixture of brambles and holly and hawthorn and nettles, ready-made for her purpose. Unwelcome barrier as it was, it prevented Danny colliding with the solid trunk of a silver birch which grew just beyond, but he had to pay a price. When he finally extricated himself from the greenery, he looked like something on which the cat had broken its claws.

"Aw Teenie," he gasped, "ye didnae need tae dae that! A've got mair thorns in ma body than a bloody porcupine an' ma face feels it's been scrubbed wi' a roadman's brush!"

"Try any mair o' yer nonsense an' ye'll wish yer faither had never been born, or yer grandfaither either!" Teenie had a delightful way of changing a stock phrase or extending it with superfluities, but the result was usually quaint enough to make it acceptable. Even to add to its import.

A truce was finally reached and operations resumed.

Soon Teenie reckoned she had a bite.

"Whit will A dae, professor?" she rasped.

"Gie it plenty o' time."

Teenie immediately started to peel yards of line off the reel, yards of line which got itself wrapped round a small bush jutting out almost horizontally from the bank. She then pulled on her rod, hoping to avert disaster, but only succeeded in tightening the nylon round the twigs and creating an almighty fankle.

"Ye're a dirty rotten devil, Danny Stook! Ye just wanted me tae loss that fish, ye snivellin' bugger. Ye kent whit wid happen when ye telt me to tae gie it plenty o' line."

"A telt ye tae gie it plenty o' *time!*"

" Ye did nut, yuh scraggy craw. Ye were frightened A wid get a fish an' you widnae. An' show ye up." Her great moon of a face looked like a traffic light - on red. Danny decided that gentle, sympathetic treatment might be the answer - it might.

"Naw, ye're wrong, Teenie. A want ye tae get a fish, A really dae. See, A'll sort oot yer line."

And as Danny was in the act of bending down to disentangle the nylon from the bush, Teenie gave vent to a most unladylike bellow:

"Right, get in there an' catch me yin then!" At the same time she brought up a massive Wellington boot and planted it with resounding force on Danny's jutting exterior. He belly-flapped into the pool, landing with his head a good 6 ft. from the edge.

Struggling and gasping, he dog-paddled to the bank and pulled himself out. He was being sorely tried and this showed in his less carefully chosen language:

"Teenie, ye're an awfu' woman! Ye must be the wildest bitch between here an' Goad knows whaur. A'm drookit an' A'm droont!"

53

Tales of Fishing and Fishermen

"Well, it's a guid way o' coolin' doon a' thae stings ye got. An' A dare say ye needed a guid wash anyway. An' watch yer language or ye'll get anither yin. C'moan, we'll get oan wi' the fishin'."

She didn't even give Danny the chance to wring some of the water from his clothes. Her cast was sorted out and in went the worm again. Her companion threw in his own just above it, and after a few moments he felt the "tug-tug" of a good trout. He struck sooner and harder than usual - and missed. But his lead weight, a steel nut of considerable dimensions, came flying out of the water like a projected missile and did not miss his fiery disciple. She received it full pelt on the bridge of her big pear-shaped conk and somehow the nylon wound itself round one ear and her red barrel of a neck.

"Tryin' tae choke me noo, ye murderin' tyke?", she screamed and made a grab for Danny, for poor Danny, who had already suffered the pain and the indignity of being pitched into thorns, then into water. As if he had not endured enough.

But, unfortunately for him, as she moved forward she trod on the line and the hook became impaled in her ample woodman's shirt which, with brass buttons pinging off in all directions, ripped down the middle, exposing a brassière-like contraption of such massive proportions that it looked as if it had been designed for twin hot-water cisterns, and equally enormous were the contents thereof.

"Christ!" thought Danny, his eyeballs as big as bubble-floats, "they're like ootsize bloody melons in canvas buckets!"

"Whit ye starin' at, ye dirty auld boar?" roared Teenie, embarrassed for perhaps the first time in her life and suddenly aware that she was exposing to the world in general and to Danny Stook in particular what must have been the biggest, and the most grotesque, bosom in Inverness-shire, if not in all Caledonia.

But she needn't have worried, for Danny's stare expressed only awe and frank disbelief rather than carnal desire. Teenie, however, was an inveterate man-hater and the slightest suggestion of any jiggery-pokery immediately raised her suspicions and put her on her very able guard.

And, following upon the pummelling Danny had already received, the sight of these gigantic impedimenta was just about enough:

"A'm feelin' dizzy, A'm gaun hame," he ventured.

"Aw, gi'en it up, are ye? Frightened A beat ye at yer ain game? Cockin' oot?"

"Ye mean *chickenin'* oot," corrected Danny. Teenie was at it again, murdering the language, twisting sayings she had heard but could never remember exactly.

"Naw, honest, Teenie, A'm feelin' fair no' weel. A'm awa' hame for a dry-oot an' a lie-doon oan ma bed."

For once Teenie showed a little compassion. Just a little...

"A' richt. A'll get ma shirt shewed up an' we'll come again the morn. Be ready the back o' nine o' clock!"

"Goad forbid!" thought Danny, then said, as convincingly as possible:

"Aye, we'll see!"

But there was a definite limit to what a human being could stand, both physically and mentally, and if he was to have any hope of survival, temporary as it might be, he knew there and then that the next day he would be as far away as possible from the river, the village, Teenie McTavish and the many attributes, to use a kinder term than they perhaps deserved, with which that charming lady was so well endowed.

Caustic Revenge

ALL THE available evidence suggested that Donald McGuire's daughter, Lorna, had been attacked, when cycling home late along the river, by a man called Alec Lawson. But it had been an exceptionally dark night and Lawson had simply denied all knowledge of the affair, providing an alibi which, if unsubstantiated, was also irrefutable. So the hair found on his clothing, hair which was almost certainly Lorna's, and other leads, such as bruises on his face, did not constitute conclusive proof - not even the words like "No!" "Help!" and "Mr. Lawson," which the police had just been able to make out amidst the mumble-jumble and intermittent groaning, in Lorna's fleeting moments of semi-consciousness. But they were proof enough for Donald McGuire, who secretly swore he would revenge this dastardly act if it was the last thing he did while still on this earth.

It was fairly common knowledge that Lawson was a poacher of salmon and that over the years he had had one or two tussles with the authorities. It was also believed, amongst those who participated in the same remunerative pastime, that he had lately abandoned his net for the more distasteful and effective cymag and that he was obtaining it from the chemical factory where he worked.

McGuire acquired this last piece of information from a sympathiser and bided his time, verifying that Lawson did in fact use cymag and furtively finding out where and how he operated. He also learned that if Lawson was convicted once more, he was likely to suffer the severest punishment.

Then the position he had been waiting for - store-keeper at the factory - came up, because the man who had held it was suspected of underhand behaviour in issuing certain supplies. McGuire applied for the post and got it, having left no stone unturned to see that he did.

Lawson, because of the nature of his job, visited the store frequently for the things he needed. McGuire watched him intently, especially when he was attending to other visitors, and on two different occasions saw him steal a tin of cymag. The new storekeeper said nothing.

A third and then a fourth tin were stolen and McGuire noticed that it always happened on a Monday, when he was at his busiest. The next time he saw Lawson approach the store on that day, he took out the end tin of the row and replaced it with another, having first scratched on it a small identifying mark. As soon as Lawson had gone, he verified that it was this tin the latter had taken.

Two nights later Lawson visited the river which was running low and in perfect condition for dosing the long, deep holding pool known as The Slipe.

He waded out into the head of the sluggish stream, up to his chest, cocked an ear to make sure all was quiet, then removed the lid from the tin. He emptied the entire contents on to the water which was only inches from his face.

The next moment, the nocturnal tranquillity of the countryside erupted to the agonising cries of someone apparently gone mad. Lawson came pounding out of the water, more by accident than judgement, because he was far beyond being capable of judging anything. His hands clutched his face and his desperate screams terrorised every living thing within a radius of half-a-mile.

In direct contrast, the face that watched from the bushes was wreathed in satisfaction. There was no regret at the obvious enormity of his revenge, no pity, no remorse, no misgivings, for his feelings towards the monster Lawson remained as caustic as the soda with which he had replaced the cymag.

McGuire glided off into the night and Lawson ran about berserk until he collided with a tree and fell unconscious.

He lay until an early morning angler found him and within an hour he was in the intensive care unit of the infirmary. All that remained of one eye was a messy smear around the socket. His face was full of holes and he had no lips.

For a week he lay hovering precariously between survival and submission. Recover he did, but the life he was destined to lead was no more than a living death, his mind having been affected as much as his body.

An accident, said the court. Lawson thought he was using cymag but wasn't. And, of course, no penalty was exacted, his self-inflicted punishment being out of all proportion to his crime.

It was six weeks later that Lorna stirred gently and for the first time came properly out of her coma. She smiled at her parents who had rushed to the infirmary on being informed of her improved condition. A fortnight later she was allowed home, her scars still ugly but disappearing. For the first time she was able to give McGuire and his wife a composed and detailed account of the happenings on that terrible night.

She now remembered that someone had come running up and driven off her attacker, carried her to a house, rung the doorbell, and disappeared. Yes, it was that poacher fellow - what was his name? Yes, Lawson! No doubt he had been after salmon and wanted his presence by the river to remain a secret. Perhaps her father would take her to see him as soon as possible so that she could express her gratitude?

Big Jake

STOORIE TAM had always managed to avoid a direct confrontation with the owner of the Ballairg Estate because he invariably crossed over from the wood before daybreak and at half-light had his appetising bunch of worms working through what he knew was by far the best throw for that type of fishing in the whole river. The dustman would usually get his salmon, or two of them, sometimes even three, within an hour, which meant that in midsummer he would recross to safety by five o'clock in the morning, before any sane laird or servants were up and about.

He was fairly cunning was Stoorie, and never abused his self-granted privilege or pushed his luck too far by staying too long or going too often. But he knew the ways of salmon, and he picked his mornings well. Hence, he was eminently successful, and the fact that his fish were poached from a member of the aristocracy seemed to add a further touch of spice.

His only real worry at such an early hour was Big Jake. The latter was a monstrous Ayrshire bull, all of 33 hundredweight, and with a temper to match. He simply hated the sight of everyone, and especially of Stoorie Tam, who dared to fish across the fence from him only because his passion for whipping out salmon exceeded his fear of the animal, but only just; and indeed, Stoorie periodically examined the fence to which Jake would often come to bellow at him and paw the ground in uncontrolled rage as he fished only 30 yds. away. He reckoned that, frightening as the din was, he was safe as long as the fence remained strong and intact, and tried to convince himself that the danger was more apparent than real.

After a drought which lasted right through June and most of July, the weather finally broke and a deluge pelted the surrounding countryside. Stoorie smacked his lips, dug his worms - and bided his time, waiting for two days to pass before rising at half-past two in the morning and wading across the broad flat above The Sack, which he knew would be brimful of fresh fish and in tip-top condition for his great writhing bait.

When it was three-quarters light, he threaded five of the monsters on to a stout No. 2 hook and cast upstream and across to bring the tantalising mass through the lie where, in such favourable conditions, he seldom failed. But there was no offer, so Stoorie took a couple of steps downstream and cast again.

This time he got well and truly hanked. He pulled and jerked in every possible direction, moving up the bank in the process, but to no avail. Then, annoyed that he was losing valuable time, he gave one mighty heave. The hook and about half the original quantity of worms came flying towards him and he had to duck smartly to avoid being hit full in the face by this fleshy missile projected by his own hand. It sped, at lightning speed, towards the fence and the field.

That morning there had been no sign of Big Jake, although Stoorie well

knew he might be lying or grazing behind the one and only hillock in the five-acre meadow and that he could come lumbering over at any second to give vent to that fiendish roaring that never failed to send ice-cold shivers up and down his spine and sometimes made him wonder if his forays were not fraught with too much risk.

Big Jake had in fact sauntered over to the fence just after Stoorie had made that second fatal cast. But he was placid and full of unusual contentment after an early breakfast of the lush grass and clover to which the recent rains had added extra sweetness. Perhaps he saw Stoorie, perhaps not, but in any case, first things first and Jake had just taken a firm stance and raised his tail, preparing to irrigate or fertilise - or perhaps both - the two square yards of ground just behind his rear legs, when the sharp No. 2 hook, which Stoorie had just ducked to avoid, impaled itself on one of the two more delicate parts of his anatomy which, with their thick discoloured skins folded and wrinkled abominably, hung like two great misshapen pears, indisputable testimony of Jake's past achievements as a sire.

In fact the locals, whose airt, it must be admitted, had produced neither men nor monuments of notable worth, thought these two massive phenomena should have figured in current books of records, alongside similar but much less spectacular items such as the largest melon or pumpkin ever grown.

As Stoorie tightened to retrieve his hook from, as he thought, soft yielding grass, Jake gave vent to a roar that echoed along the line of hills and sent flocks of rooks scurrying from their perches in raucous panic. With his tail still held high, and the effluent of the previous evening's grazing streaming out behind him, he went off at a gallop. Then his eye fell on Stoorie, who was standing there as if moonstruck, with his line screaming from his reel. The great bull wheeled towards this familiar and deeply-loathed figure who was no doubt the cause of his sudden and unexpected agony. Stoorie, fence or not, dropped everything and flew towards the shallow flat, crossing it so fast that his feet hardly seemed to break the surface.

Meanwhile, Jake was pounding towards what was now a very fragile barrier and, having reached this obstacle which stood between him and his quarry, he swung round with his great, broad hindquarters and three stout posts snapped off at ground level as if they had been bamboo canes in a garden plot.

Jake plunged into The Stack but could see his sworn enemy was leaping the dry stane dyke into the wood on the other side and, realising in a clumsy sort of way that further pursuit was useless, he stood in the pool up to his middle and let the sweet, cool river water soothe the dirty, nagging wound he had been dealt.

Tales of Fishing and Fishermen

Needless to say, it was the first time the local vet, or perhaps any vet for that matter, had been summoned to remove from the testicle of an Ayrshire bull a No. 2 hook still strung with some severed and bedraggled earthworms.

For seemingly endless months, Stoorie suffered horrific nightmares in which he was chased by bellowing, fire-spitting bulls the size of dinosaurs which threw great iron fences into the sky as if they were fashioned from sticks and string.

Then came what appeared to be momentous news. Stoorie heard in the village pub that Big Jake had been struck by lightning and was dead.

Yes, Big Jake was dead and it had taken a double flash to kill him. But Stoorie's jubilation was short-lived, because Jake was almost immediately replaced in the same meadow by one of his sons who, although only two years old, already showed he would match or even excel the gigantic proportions of his father. From what Stoorie heard, the youngster had also been endowed with his old man's fiery temper, only more so, and that was enough for the dustman, who thought the chances were high that the animal might also have inherited an incalculable hatred for a certain person who, with a bunch of worms, liked to take salmon from a certain private pool very early in the morning.

Stoorie remembered his awful nightmares and resigned himself to the inevitable. Never again did his colossal bait bump its way enticingly down the salmon-rich bed of The Sack.

Salmy Salara

PERHAPS every natural species produces, on extremely rare occasions, an individual which is endowed with superior gifts or intelligence, a freak, a biological error.

And so it was with Salmy Salara. Salmy had first seen the light of day, as it filtered through his yolk-sac, in a burn high in the Cairngorms. While still very young he obtained his food much more easily than his mates because he learned more quickly than they which eddies were apt to trap juicy particles and which were not. He became the leader of a shoal and as he grew bigger and moved downstream and into the great river, he had plenty of camp followers trailing in his wake. By now a beautifully-proportioned parr and large for his age, he heard the irresistible call and made for estuary and ocean - still pursued by his retinue of protégés, suddenly turned silver like himself.

But once the rich feeding-grounds had been reached, far off in the chilly seas of the North-West, the hangers-on finally forsook him, there being no longer any need for them to forage. Salmy himself sucked and chewed to his heart's content and grew rapidly. The months went past:12.....24.....36.

Then came a second call, the great call home, and Salmy, now almost 3 ft. long, thick-set and bursting with vitality, answered it willingly. He crossed the boundless ocean in record time, then slowed and nosed his way into the estuary of the great salmon river whose little tributary had cradled him as a fingerling.

Heavy rain the previous day had produced a fine flow of water and Salmy was able to move steadily upstream. Some of his fellows who had been waiting just off-shore and had tagged on behind him had got themselves trapped in the greedy nets festooning the murky tidal water, but he, apparently using some strange gift denied to them, had managed to take successful evasive action and enter the river unmolested.

A couple of days later, now 10 miles upstream and tenanting what, unknown to him, was one of the choice fishing beats, his attention was arrested by an attractive-looking morsel crossing the current just a foot in front of his nose. Feeling in a playful mood, he moved after it and sucked it in. He then made to move back to the spot he had occupied but was aware of some resistance. It reminded him of the thick mass of seaweed he had had to plough through when he had entered the estuary.

He noted that if he pulled downstream, against the pressure, the distance between himself and this strange creature increased until the latter also moved down, winding something as he did so. Therefore, deciding to get further away from this creature which seemed to have more than a little to do with his predicament, he turned round and made quickly for the tail of the pool. And then, as he felt the surge of the fast water at the head of the

Tales of Fishing and Fishermen

next stream he decided to let it take him with it - and suddenly the pressure was gone. He felt a slight annoyance in his left jaw but so small as to be of little consequence.

Salmy went back to his lie, surfaced and had a peep at the other world. The creature was stooping, apparently busy with something.

The following day the creature again appeared and Salmy, still with the salt of the sea in his veins and ready for a game, took the bright offering once more. Then he let the creature play with him for some time and, when he had become a little bored with it all, he indulged in his downstream act and brought the proceedings to an end. Once again he was aware of a not-too-pleasant sensation in his mouth but it did little to detract from the fun.

The next day Salmy, feeling a trifle restless, pushed on upstream and stopped for a while on a stretch of river that seemed to be bristling with the same type of creature he had already encountered. Looking for further diversion he in turn seized, and broke off, the playthings offered by three of these creatures all standing within a few feet of each other. He noted that they all seemed to have become very active, pointing to where Salmy had seized each of their bright toys and making his surroundings reverberate unpleasantly as their mouths opened and closed at great speed.

As he reached the headwaters, Salmy gradually found himself in the company of more and more of his own kind. But when they grasped one of those titbits that tantalisingly crossed the current they didn't know how to react and after much pulling and running and splashing and twisting, they were generally hauled from the river, never to return.

Salmy decided to lay on a demonstration. He took what in fact was a large Mepps and showed how easy it was to break free of the creature on the bank. The new game became all the rage in the upper pools of the river.

It goes without saying that there was rage of a different kind - and absolute consternation - amongst the creatures who wielded sticks and filled the water with attractive morsels like worms and Stoat's Tails and Grey Monkeys and Black and Golds and Yellow Bellies. Over a period of eight weeks - until the season ended - 73 salmon were hooked in a string of five consecutive pools and only six of them landed - all fresh fish which had just arrived and, therefore, uninitiated into escape tactics by the efficient tutor Salmy.

Time wore on. Salmy, the salmon extraordinary, spawned but returned, more massive than ever, the following season to cause further havoc and bewilderment amongst the angling fraternity. But that winter, one cold December morning, when he spewed forth his milt for the second time, he also lost his life-blood and was no more.

Those he had instructed on his first and second visits and who had survived to return yet again were lacking in the bizarre attribute he had possessed and so were incapable of passing on his teachings to those arriving for the first time.

And those of the old anglers of the headwaters who are still with us talk frequently, in subdued tones tinged with awe, about the two seasons when everything went haywire, when nothing made sense.

Catching them is easy

DUGGIE RENWICK, armed with his faithful old split-cane, oft-repaired but still sweet-functioning spinning reel and inevitable can of worms, and wearing a jerkin and corduroys, both of which bore such a multitude of diversely-coloured patches that it was difficult to tell where one garment ended and the other began, was striding out eagerly towards The Alders soon after daybreak when he suddenly stopped in his tracks. Judging by the amount of equipment lying about it looked, from a distance, as if campers had invaded the banks and, if there was anything Duggie hated to see by a river, it was tents and people and the unholy mess many of them trailed in their wake.

But his irritation soon developed into downright annoyance when, on getting nearer, he saw that it was a one-man outfit, an earlier arrival, who was surrounded by all the paraphernalia that the tackle industry could concoct. He cursed, because visitors usually hogged the brackish pools down by the sea, where uncatchable fish were always showing.

Accustomed as he was to seeing over-equipped visiting anglers, Duggie stopped and stared aghast at the amount and diversity of the armament the intruder had in his possession: two fly rods and reels, a spinning rod and reel, two landing nets of different sizes, a huge square-shaped basket that would have held a small man, never mind a large salmon; and a game-bag, a picnic outfit with oil stove and, arrayed beneath a gigantic red and yellow parasol, two large plastic trays, one of which seemed to display every size and pattern of fly (known and hitherto unknown), while the other was filled to the brim with minnows and spoons and what have you of every hue and shape and size, and inlaid with little bowl-shaped containers over-flowing with swivels, beads and anti-kink devices. There were, in addition, bobbins of nylon of a dozen different breaking strains, a couple of books on tactics, a priest, a hook extractor, a thermometer, a set of scales and a camera. And the stranger's hat and lapels held enough flies to stock a reasonably-sized fishing tackle shop for a season or two. Emblazoned on his blazer badge in bright pink letters were the words: *FLY FISHERS OF MILWAUKEE.*

When Duggie's senses became unnumbed, he wondered how the stranger had ever succeeded in negotiating the rough terrain encumbered with such a mountainous load. Perhaps, he mused, he had dropped from an aeroplane, using the enormous parasol as a parachute? And he tittered at his own joke.

Mincing words had never been one of Duggie's faults. On reaching the intruder, who bore the name Bartholomew Potts, he ejaculated:

"Michty me, I didna ken the Game Fair was being held here this mornin'!"

"Just because I have equipment which is vastly superior to your own, there is no need to be sarcastic, my man. *Toujours la politesse!*"

"Listen, codger, dinnae come it wi' me. I've seen your kind before, aye laden wi' everything but **FISH**! I've a big bag tae but I prefer to fill it wi' somethin' worthwhile!"

"You don't expect me to believe that you catch fish with that clumsy old stick you have? Envy is a terrible thing!"

"Aye, an' ignorance is worse! Man, I'm heart sorry for ye. If ye kent onything aboot fishin' ye widna be cairryin' a' that useless junk aboot wi' ye!"

"Know nothing about fishing? My dear man, I'll have you know I've just attended an expensive course in the States and have been coached in both style and tactics by the best instructors in the whole world (which entitles me to wear this proud badge), and have in addition been given the opportunity to purchase some of the latest and most effective lures, available only to those attending the course. For example, do you see that fly in the corner of the tray? It has every imaginable colour of feather and hair, all natural materials and none of them dyed, also the most brilliant gold and silver tinsel you could ever find. It's quite unique, a work of art. Do you know what it's called?"

Duggie rubbed his eyes as he tried to focus on the gaudy two-inch monster: "Bird o' Paradise? Feather Duster?" he suggested.

"Oh, I didn't know there were such flies. I thought I had them all. I must get some. No, it's called the Dakota Cocktail and is a renowned killer."

"I dare say, I can imagine ony salmon seein' that wid dee o' heart failure. Hivens man, this is supposed tae be a river, no' a shootin' stall at the fair!"

But Bartholomew Potts was not to be daunted:

"Here is something else, the very latest and the very best in sophisticated minnows. Look at it - it costs 12 dollars, and apart from its wonderful psychedelic colours, it has a tiny motor which makes it zigzag and dive and leap a foot out of the water every few yards."

"Ye'll better watch it disna flee awa'," came the cynical retort. "If auld Jock McNab sees that he'll think its a fleein' fish an' blast it wi' his shotgun. Haw! Haw!"

"You know, my man, I never cease to be amazed - and distressed, I can assure you - by the stupid obstinacy of people like yourself. You don't move with the times and you would rather go and dig filthy worms and fish with them than utilise all the wonderful new patterns and revolutionary gadgets that modern expertise has put at our disposal."

"Hiv' ye feenished yer sermon, then? Fur Goad's sake stop it!" pleaded Duggie. Then he went on:

"But jist tell me this! Wha invented the worm? It strikes me it moves better o' its ain accord than ony o' thae silly-lookin' things you're cairryin' aboot. An' worms dinna cost 12 dollars each."

At that moment a salmon, and then a grilse, showed towards the far bank. Duggie hastened to get his tackle ready but the visitor had had a fair start on

Tales of Fishing and Fishermen

him and plunged into the pool with his spinning rod and Leapin' Lu, as he termed it.

But the garish device was not infallible, not that morning at any rate. Admittedly it made its presence felt in that a moorhen and two ducks took off backwards and one of the latter walloped bottom first into a gorse bush, which only served to add to its agonised cries. Then great beams were seen cutting downstream towards the shallows at the head of the next pool as salmon fled, in unashamed panic, to seek the sanctuary of saner waters. Duggie kept to the stream at the top, floating his worms down the far bank and into the deep, short lie unknown to the visitor and several yards upstream of him.

A salmon took the bait in the usual worm-taking manner and ran fast for the head of the pool. Then, when Duggie "gave it the butt," it turned round in its own length and, flashing like a sleek, silver torpedo, it tore back downstream. Bartholomew Potts, oblivious to what was going on, and wondering, desperately, why his gorgeous Leapin' Lu had not already been seized by a grateful salmon, was in the act of casting out the nightmarish contraption yet again. It landed right in the path of Duggie's salmon and the fish, confronted with this hellish concoction performing its crazy acrobatics a mere couple of feet before its very eyes, stopped dead in its tracks, reared up on its tail and turned through 180 degrees at such scintillating speed that Duggie just could not cope and in a matter of seconds his line hung limp and tangled round his top-piece like a piece of badly-mangled wire-netting.

"Ye damned nuisance, ye!" he roared at Bartholomew Potts. "See whit ye've din' wi' yer Leapin' Loonie or Yakota Docktail or whitever ye ca' it. Ye've cost me a guid fish, ye hiv. Awa' an' tak' a' that rubbish oot o' here before I send fur the Purification Board!"

"Wait a minute, my dear chap, you're not trying to tell me you hooked that fish legitimately - with worm? And they were refusing my Leapin' Lu! It's incredible!"

"Look mate, hoo dae ye think I learnt tae fish? I learnt here on the water by watchin' and listenin' tae the auld yins when I was a wee laddie, then tryin' it masel'. Ma auld faither caught mair salmon wi' the worm than you've ever seen, or ever wull see, an' I started catchin' them before I was 14, efter aboot four years at the troots. Since then I've caught 2,126 salmon." Then he added wryly: "An' it should be 2,127."

The intruder stared, agape. He hadn't caught any.

"It's jist that ye hivna' been brocht up the richt way," Duggie went on to explain in kinder tones, which were born of an idea that had just struck him. "If ye ever hope tae be a fisher ye'll hiv' tae git rid o' encumbrances an' git doon tae bare essentials. Ye've got tae concentrate on yin or twa ways o' fishin' an' git tae ken them inside oot.

"Noo the best way tae catch salmon in ony size o' water is wi' the worm, the big, blackheedit gairden worm. A' ye need is a flee rod - because it's longer than a spinnin' rod an' fishes the worm better, a spinnin' reel, a guid, strong line an' big single hooks.

"Nane o' that load o' trash is necessary - it jist huds ye back. Noo if ye want tae be a fisher ye'll hiv' tae mak' a clean sweep an' start again at the beginnin'. Jist you watch me!"

Duggie then proceeded to give a practical demonstration of his prowess, casting his worms across and upstream and letting line fly from his reel so that the bait sank immediately before beginning to drift slowly down through the lie. He prayed and prayed that a salmon would take him, and take him one did. He gave a running commentary on its behaviour and his own reactions to it, and finally, as the fish raced upstream and crashed to the surface he yelled:

"Ye tighten intae him noo!"

The salmon was duly coaxed on to the gravel and slid well back from the edge. It was a thickset, gleaming beauty of 12 lb.

"Tell ye whit," said Duggie, "you hiv' this as a present. I can git plenty mair. An' if ye say ye caught it yersel' I'll no be hearin' ye."

Bartholomew Potts was flabbergasted.

"You mean it's for me? Are you sure?"

"Tell ye whit," continued Duggie, "if ye like I'll tak a' that rubbish awa' and burn it in ma smiddy fire an' then there'll be nothin' tae stop ye catching salmon the next time ye come, noo that I've shown ye hoo tae dae it, like."

"Fine, fine. Yes, you go ahead and burn the lot."

When the stranger had gone off in jubilant mood with the salmon, Duggie tossed the abandoned Dakota Cocktails and Leapin' Lus, together with a host of other eccentricities, into his own bag and carried them off to the smiddy. He carried them to the smiddy, but they did not end up in the forge.

When Bartholomew Potts had gone back home, Duggie went down to the estuary, which was still busy with visiting anglers trying to entice those uncatchable salmon which were always showing there in tantalising fashion. He spread out his wares on the short grass and acclaimed in enthusiastic tones the great virtues of Dakota Cocktails and Leapin' Lus and Tennessee Terrors and Irresistible Magnets. They were expensive, of course, but a real investment, as they could almost be claimed to be infallible.

He did a roaring trade and was gone before Sergeant McIver had taken his morning stroll through the village.

Then he went home and threw the few remaining unsold lures into his furnace, perhaps partly to ease his conscience, and got out his old rod and reel and worms. And within an hour number 2,127 had become number 2,129.

Another Night to Remember

It WAS WITH feverish excitement, unashamed and unconcealed, that the stalwarts of the Doonieburnie Angling Club looked forward to their Twenty-third Annual Social Evening. Previous gatherings had always taken place in the austere and drafty and dilapidated village hall (whose roof, according to carpenter Shugh Tarff, was held up by cobwebs and would collapse if they had one more dry summer), with a local caterer, knowing that he could get away with gastronomic murder, usually offering a menu of which the main ingredients were pease brose, haggis and neeps and rhubarb and custard. But Secretary Seamus Murdoch, always with a propensity for momentous decision-taking, whether it was to increase the annual re-stocking of the Doonie by an extra dozen 8-inch trout or to use the same sum to get repairs done to the bottom step of the fishing hut, had risen to unprecedented heights by persuading his committee to let him arrange that year's social in the sumptuous new motel at the head of the glen, invitingly named *Le Paradis* by its French-born owner. A cronie of Seamus' wife's cousin's auntie had got a job there as a cleaner and the glowing reports she brought back made Seamus determined to give his members another night to remember. After all, the daily pattern of their lives was characterised more by hard toil and sweat that the *dolce vita,* and it was not often they could be given a taste of the heavenly bliss which the very name of the establishment seemed to promise.

So a variegated convoy, led by Seamus on his ancient motorbike (propelled by one part petrol and three parts paraffin) and consisting of the local garage's rickety old bus, a couple of tractors pulling bogeys (scraped more or less clean of what they usually transported) and one or two bicycles belonging to those who preferred it the hard way, assembled at the Village Cross and, on Seamus' word of command, set off in a blare of hooters and a blaze of lights and blue smoke. They banged and rattled and snorted their way up the side of the Doonie, their beloved Doonie, now out of bounds for the season and apparently celebrating its freedom from their attentions as it roared down in raucous, carefree flood, perhaps mirroring the temperament of its habitués who, that very night, were hell-bent on enjoying to the full all the amenities and pleasures offered by the glittering new edifice where they were paying more for four or five hours' entertainment than they normally spent on self-indulgence in as many months.

On arrival they made a bee-line for the lounge, having been carefully instructed by Seamus in a briefing the previous evening that they must buy at least one drink each, for the sake of a protocol with which they were quite unfamiliar. Seamus knew he could hardly expect more, because to a man, the Doonieburnians had been only too well informed by the cronie of Seamus' wife's cousin's auntie of the high cost, in *Le Paradis*, of the malt whisky of

Another Night to Remember

which they were all passionately fond and he was well aware they would come well stocked with their own home-made but excellent brand. For large inside pockets were ideal places for concealing flat-shaped half-bottles and flasks and the first glass, the cost of which made many of them fervently wish they were back in the village hall with its cobweb-supported roof and its fodder, was surreptitiously and frequently replenished from the secret containers, so that by the time Seamus announced, in his poshest tones, that dinner was ready and they were to follow him into the dining-room, the scene was irrevocably set for unprecedented incidents born of unprecedented behaviour. Monsieur Berberac may have owned establishments not only in Paris, but in Biarritz and Casablanca and Rome, but he had never had guests before who, en masse, were to exhibit, both in speech and action, such a degree of uninhibited conduct. The stultifying effects of city life and the mass media, with their tendency to obliterate individual personalities and to cast everyone in the same monotonous mould, had so far made little headway in the remote glen of the Doonie, still a haven of naturalness where social taboos were simply non-existent and, as Sammy Sinclair was wont to say, where nobody would think twice about it if the minister, for want of something more acceptable, cleaned his perpetually running nose by drawing it along his sleeve.

When the procession reached the resplendent dining-room, with its thick, lush carpeting, and candlelit tables and subdued wall lighting, with slim-hipped, cummerbunded waiters hovering discreetly in the background, fiery wee man-hater Lizzie Glen (readers will recall the incident concerning her in "A Night to Remember") was the first to give an inkling of what was to come. The first lady to enter, she was promptly taken by the arm by a well-meaning waiter who intended ushering her to a table. But to Lizzie a mere touch from a man, quite irrespective of the circumstances, was like a sting from a viper and the helpful Algerian was sent on his way, wherever that was, with a lightning jab from the elbow accompanied, almost instantaneously, by a searing blow in the shin from a hefty brogue:

"Ye dirty French boar!" she yelled. To Lizzie all men were boars - and boars in heat.

The other waiters stared askance, perplexed and hesitant, and when 18-stone Teenie McTavish swashbuckled in to reverberating candelabra, her great bull-like face a belligerent mixture of red and purple and her mighty front heaving like a monstrous pair of buoys in a storm-tossed sea, the elegant team of waiters pressed themselves tighter against the wall. . .

Then, when everyone was seated and a sign had been given by Monsieur Bergerac, they converged silently, but perhaps a little gingerly, on the tables to distribute massive gold-rimmed menus to the diners.

69

Tales of Fishing and Fishermen

Wee Davy Craw, who had decided to leave his dentures at home as he was always losing them anyway, each time he coughed or sneezed, ejecting them, because of their ill-fitting slackness, into places like bowls of custard, when they usually ended up as an unexpected addition to someone else's sweet course, took the large proffered card and stared agog. Davy had quite a task on his hands each time he tried to read everyday English, but to be confronted with this incomprehensible jargon was akin to having to decipher a highly complicated code. Not knowing it was in fact a menu and wondering why it had been handed to him, he asked his neighbour, old Billy Howker, what on earth he was supposed to do as the waiter was obviously expecting some reaction.

"It's mebbe tae pit the teapot oan when it comes - ye ken, yin o' thae mat things tae keep the table frae bein' burnt," was the best veteran Billy could offer.

The waiter, who had served in eating-houses of world-wide repute, showed visible signs of growing impatience. Then he ventured:

"Would you like to order, Monsieur? What will you have to whet your palate?"

Davy was familiar neither with the accent nor the phraseology:

"Eh? Wet ma plate? Whit fur? An' mak' ma tatties a' soggy when A get them?"

But, aware that these surroundings were foreign soil to him and recalling Seamus' instructions of the night before and not wishing to appear unco-operative, he proceeded to grab a water jug and to pour some of its contents into his still empty plate. He then looked expectantly at the waiter who, mesmerised and confused and at a complete loss, ran to Monsieur Berberac for succour and advice.

As this general pattern of mutual miscomprehension and bewilderment was developing at every table, Seamus was approached by the proprietor to see if the "peasants present" - Monsieur Bergerac was now becoming somewhat less polite - could be asked there and then to make their choice.

Seamus, by no means a gourmet himself and no more experienced than the others in banqueting in high places, realised it was his duty to establish his authority and to make things run more smoothly. So, holding the menu six inches from his face, and using the huge magnifying glass which he always kept handy for tricky jobs such as this, he commenced:

"Noo, folks, listen cairfully. This here caird is tae tell us whit we can huv' fur oor denner. Ye choose yin thing frae the first five because there's a row o' stars under them an' that means the next lot is the second thing ye ate."

This lucid explanation was greeted with a stunned silence. Then Dunky Todd, whose presence at meetings was appreciated by everyone because of his penchant for asking pertinent questions, always putting in clear unambiguous terms thoughts which others were quite unable to express, asked:

"Can ye no' get it a' oan the yin plate? Then it widnae a' get cauld."

"Noo, Dunky, dinnae be sae stupit. The plates wid be too heavy tae cairry if they did it like that. Noo, folks, please tell thae waiter chaps whit ye huv' choosed."

"It diznae mak' nae sense," roared roadman Sanny Naismith, "It looks mair like a list o' thae fitba' teams that comes tae Glesca noo an' again. A like tae ken whit's gaun doon ma thrapple. We could a' get pishioned!"

"Noo, noo, Sanny, ye like a bit o' fish, dae ye no'? Well, whit's wrang wi' the *Salmon Mousse?*"

"*Salmon Moose? Salmon Moose?* Salmon's a'richt, bit moose wi' it? Whit a bloody mixture! Wha ye kiddin'? Listen, A've picked the odd moose oot o' ma porridge because this skinflint wife o' mine will no gaun intae a grocer's if she can help it - she gets the oats fur ma porridge sweepin' them up frae the barn flair at the croft whaur she gauns fur tae buy cheap auld tatties. Ye can keep yer *Salmon Moose.*"

The irate Mrs. Naismith, who, in her own reckoning, was the epitome of the efficient housewife and cook, proceeded to thump her husband's huge red nose against the ornate table-cloth. Davy Craw, sitting on his other side, seized the opportunity to rid himself of his water-filled plate by swapping it for Sanny's.

About the same time, a dapper little waiter, sincerely wishing to be of assistance, leaned over Sam McKendrick and ran his forefinger along one of the items on the menu, at which Sam was staring as if hypnotised. He pronounced it "velly good".

"Whit? *Pimply moose?*" bellowed Sam. Ye tryin' tae mak' a fool o' me? A'll clout ye wan, ye wee French puddock, ye!"

"But *Pamplemousse* velly, velly good to get appetite for meal."

"*Pimply moose?* Are you suggestin' A'm a bloody cat? M-i-a-o-w! Scram, before A claw yer bloody een oot."

Danny Stook, always one for grabbing whatever he thought had the greatest bulk, announced that his considered choice was *Cuisses de Grenouille avec des Escargots de Bourgogne.* The waiter smiled, thinking he had at last found someone appreciative of two of France's finest delicacies, and brought the order. As Danny was wolfing it down, he reappeared and said happily:

"I am glad to see Monsieur is enjoying so much his frogs' legs and snails."

Danny turned white and there was one mighty explosion as the total contents of his mouth, which had been full to the point of inducing lockjaw, were jettisoned with tremendous force towards the diner opposite him, none

Tales of Fishing and Fishermen

other than Slugger Thompson, who at that moment was busy slucking back, from a full plate which was held high and tipped almost to the vertical, some watery consommé which he had expected to be real kale. Slugger had been in many a fight - indeed scrapping had been his way of life - and he wasn't slow to accept the challenge. He laid his plate on the table, then, slowly and deliberately, lifted a knife, scraped the snails and frogs' legs from his front and wafted them out of his hair, all the time staring at Danny with a dead-pan expression and without blinking an eye - an ominous sign to those who knew him. Then, once he was satisfied that his clothes and person were as clean as they needed to be for the time being, he picked up his still fairly full plate, placed it carefully in his massive right paw and, with dexterous aim, leaned forward to plant both it and its contents over Danny's tortured countenance. The latter, thinking his world was coming to a premature end and not wishing to hasten the event by engaging in physical struggle with the redoubtable Slugger, said nothing, wiped his face on the table cloth and took an extra-large swig from his concealed bottle of Darlin' Doonie.

Somehow or other, the *hors d'oeuvres* were ordered and either reluctantly and even painfully consumed or stealthily pushed into places where they went unnoticed and discovered only when someone groped for his tobacco pouch or tin of shag. Often there were outbreaks of hilarious laughter, or moans of anguish, as these rough and ready sons of the glen wrested with concoctions they chose from the sound of their names which, after all, was practically the only means at their disposal.

As the fish course was somehow got through and time for the main course approached, a new band of sprightly wine waiters came forward, having been first of all warned by their colleagues of the difficulties they were likely to encounter.

Trabbie Tulloch was the first to cause a commotion, most of the ladies having opted for a Chablis which one of them knew from the empties she had seen in the mansion where she cleaned up after parties. Trabbie, of course, was not well enough experienced in places of *haute cuisine* to know that he was being accosted by a wine waiter. In fact he thought it was a request to know what he wanted for his next course.

"Would you like to order, Monsieur?"

"Aw, A dinnae ken whit tae get."

"Well, sir, we have some very fine *Beaunes*, 1963, just arrived the other day from France."

"Bones, auld French bones? An' wha's or whit's bones? Aw, Seamus, maun, whit fur in Goad's name did ye bring us here? They're a' daft. Dafter than wee hill-burn troots."

"It's you that's daft, Trabbie. That maun is askin' ye whit ye want tae drink."

"Well hoo dae ye drink bones? Jist tell me that!"

"It must be a kind o' wine, Trabbie. Try it maun!"

"Nae fears, no' while A've still got some o' this stuff in ma flask."

And pulling his container from an inside pocket, he poured half its remaining contents down his throat:

"That's whit ye ca' a drink. Bones be damned!"

When orders for the main course were being taken "Hand-Me-Down-The Moon" McCann, always keen to experiment in things both culinary and piscatorial (with regard to the latter he used fresh roe, fried roe, poached roe, boiled roe, grilled roe and even pickled roe) was attracted by the term *Cervelle de Mouton* and expected some form of mutton to which he was very partial - local hill farmers often thought of him when one of their sheep went missing - and ordered accordingly. When a waiter let it slip to Henny McNab that it was in fact sheep's brains that his neighbour was consuming with more than a little relish, Henny succumbed to fits of uncontrolled laughter:

"Hey, Canny, A ken ye huvnae mauny of yer ain an' A suppose even a sheep's brains wid be a big help tae ye!"

"Whit ye mean?"

"Jist whit A'm sayin'. That's an auld ram's heid ye're tearin' apairt and shovellin' doon yer throat!"

Six-foot-seven-and-a-half Canny's reaction was to shoot out an arm that looked like a long, mechanical shovel and ram a goodly part of the delicacy into Henny's wide-open mouth. "Well, if that's the case, ye could dae wi' some yersel. Swallow that or A'll bang yer heid off the ceilin'."

They eventually arrived at the dessert, by which time all the waiters were half-demented and morosely asking themselves and each other if this was to be the way of things on a certain evening each October. But after more miscomprehensions, verbal scuffles and guffaws and giggles, delicacies such as *Passion Fruit Fluff* and *Banana Bavarois* and *Almond Horseshoes* were eventually ordered and either guzzled or nibbled - or completely rejected. The waiters sighed with relief when the meal ended and Seamus dragged himself, perhaps a little apprehensively, to his feet:

"Well, folks, A think ye'll a' agree we huv din ye fair prood!"

"Ye've **din** us a' richt," squawked farmhand Caw-Caw Candless. "A've nivir seen sae much muck since A dunged 90 acres last winter."

"Noo, noo, Caw-Caw, son, if yer tastes are o' sic a low standard A cannae help that. It's a matter o' breedin', A suppose. A appreciated it. An' some o' us like tae get oor heids oot o' the troch noo an' again, ye ken."

"Dinna tell a lot o' lees. A saw ye turnin' green when ye tried tae ate that

Tales of Fishing and Fishermen

funny first thing ye had," croaked Caw-Caw in that deep, rough and resonant voice so reminiscent of the tones heard in the vicinity of the rookery at Auld Brig' o' Pauchle. "Ye're jist tryin' tae mak' excooses fur bringin' us tae this bloody nuthoose."

But Seamus refused to become any more involved and went on:

"Noo, noo, folks, let us get oan wi' oor presentations. This year the prize fur the heaviest fush gauns into the deservin' haunds o' oor guid freend Jockie Broon fur the 23-punder he got oan the ninth o' September oot o' the Kalepot."

"Is that whit he telt ye? Oot o' the Kalepot? He got it oot o' an otter's mooth. A saw him makin' a dive at the otter that hud jist poo'd the fush oan tae the gravel jist efter daylicht. A even saw the otter rinnin' awa'!" These illuminating remarks came from a livid Danny Stook.

"Whit bloody lees! An otter? It was a broon collie dug oot huntin' rabbits," screeched Jockie, "an' Seamus said it wiz a luvely fush, a real credit tae me, wi' no' a mark oan it. Oany stupit bugger kens an otter wid huv' left teeth marks in it."

"Aye, but ye got yer missus tae shew it a' up wi' a needle an' threed an' Seamus is gettin' sae blind he couldnae see the stitches."

Although the waiters who were still hovering about hardly understood a single word of this highly intellectual dialogue, so rich in nuances and subtlety of expression, the countenances and gesticulations of the participants alone was enough to make it into some sort of unrehearsed and quite unexpected comedy act. Other employees, put in the picture by tittering colleagues, sneaked back, under a variety of pretences, into the dining-room. After all, they were due some entertainment after all the torture they had had to endure throughout the meal.

"C'moan noo, Danny," beseeched Seamus. "Nae mair o' that! Will Jockie Broon please step oot here fur tae receive his prize!"

Jockie swaggered or rather, staggered, out to the table, to become the recipient of a long, narrow, mysterious-looking parcel.

"Well, open it!" encouraged Seamus. "Everybody will want tae see whit ye huv' got. A choosed it masel'!"

All eyes were focused on the parcel, on Jockie's clumsy fingers as he struggled unsuccessfully to undo the well-tied knots. Finally, seething with impatience, his hand flew to his side. He pulled out a sheath-knife and pieces of string shot off in all directions. Excitedly he began to rip the paper apart, certain this was the new rod he was hoping for. He certainly needed one.

A distinct hush fell on all those present when he got rid of all the wrappings to reveal his award. He stared at it, then held it aloft, his face a painful mixture of disbelief, supreme disappointment and, eventually, undisguised fury.

"Whit the hell's this? A long stick wi' a strap oan the end? Whit's this got tae dae wi' fishin'? Whit fur did ye pick this fur ma hard-airned prize, ye bloody stupit dunkey! Whit is it oanyway?"

"Man, Jockie, ye're awfu' ignorant. Dae ye no' ken that that's an expensive wadin' stick, made oot o' the best spruce that sillar can buy? Ye can wade far mair easy in coorse water if ye hud oan tae yin o' thae. The toffs has thae things, maun!"

"D-Din-Dinnae be d-d-daft, S-Seamus," - the contributor was "Machine-Gun" Massie, who spat his words out like saliva-coated bullets and had missed the previous social because his whippet had chosen that very night to produce a record litter. "J-Jock-Jockie gits a' his f-f-fu-fush oot o' the S-St-Stew-Stewpot off the b-b-bank. He's n-niver h-h-hud w-waders in his life, only t-t-t-tack-tackety b-bits. He w-widnae k-ken wh-whit tae dae wi- them."

Henny McNab, sitting opposite "Machine-Gun" and, therefore, in the direct line of fire, spluttered out that he was half-drowned, but managed to dry his bespattered face by rubbing it along his neighbour's sleeve.

"A ken whit A'll dae wi' that stick if ye dinnae rin oot o' ammoonition. A'll wrap it roond thae rhubarb blades ye huv' f-f-fur l-l-lugs." Either the habit was catching, or pint-sized Jockie was trying to ape "Machine-Gun's" speech defect.

"Aw richt, aw richt!" interrupted Seamus. "Oanyway, the stick micht encourage Jockie tae get waders. A ken that Canny hiz an auld pair that he's willin' tae sell fur a bawbee or twa."

"There ye go again," retorted Jockie. "A telt ye ye were as thick in the heid as Big Teenie is roond the waist an' that's whit ye ca' thick. Hoo can A get Canny's waders oan, wi' him aboot six feet echt an' me takin' a' ma time tae mak' five feet? A wid need tae wear bloody stults an' then that wadin' stick wid be too short. A widnae be able tae cast because A wid be stanin' there like a hauf-shut knife tryin' tae get the stick on the bottom o' the water. An' oanyway, A've seen Canny's best waders an' they're sae covered wi' rubber patches they look like black an' red checket troosers. So that diznae sae much fur his auld yins."

But Jockie should have know better than talk so disparagingly of Teenie McTavish. In fact, the outsize lady had been remarkably quiet all evening, probably because even the most foolhardy, fearing her undeniable powers of awe-inspiring counter-attack, had gone out of their way not to bait her unnecessarily. But Jockie's reckless remark was just the spark needed to light the fuse fixed to what was a human keg of gunpowder. She let him finish talking and then:

"Ye wee, humphy-backed bauchle, Ah've seen the cat bring hame better than you," she thundered. She rushed headlong from her seat, moving her massive bulk with incredible speed and agility, to grab wee Jockie by the collar and lift him effortlessly from the floor as if he had been a mere bottle of her favourite stout. She dumped him face down with resounding force on the table right in front of Seamus, picked up the wading-stick and proceeded to tan his seat as she sometimes did with her own unruly bairns. Jockie screamed for mercy and Seamus implored her to stop. This she did, but only to smash the stick to smithereens as she brought it into flashing contact with her own tremendous thighs. The pieces were then hurled angrily on to the table right in front of the Secretary himself:

"Noo ye'll no' need waders or stults nur nuthin' else!" she stormed.

Seamus clasped his hands as if in prayer. "Please, Teenie, please, gaun back tae yer seat."

Teenie glowered at him and if looks could have pulverised, he would have shrivelled away to dust. But, satisfied she had righted the great wrong she had been done, she ambled back to her place, a living warning of what was likely to happen to anyone who dared to get entangled with Mistress Teenie McTavish.

Seamus, with some of his normal verve drained out of him and having to make a superhuman effort to appear his usual enthusiastic self, went on:

"Noo, the heaviest troot wiz took by a grand caster o' a flee an' it turned the scales at $3^1/_4$ pund. It wiz yin o' the brawest troots that's ever come oot o' the Pauchle an' a' credit tae the maun that catched it oan a wee hame-made Bed Louse. Fur the second year runnin', step oot here, Bert McCann!"

"A canna believe ma ears!" roared Wullie Huntly. "Did ye no' see it wiz a rainbow troot an' ye ken fine there's nane o' them in the Pauchle. He stole it frae that fish ferm o'er at Tauschentuch."

"Ye dirty luttle tyke, ye!" screeched "Hand-Me-Down-The-Moon," shooting out a lengthy tentacle to seize Wullie by his ample coiffure and lift him screaming from his seat. "Whit did ye say?"

"A-A said it wiz a bigger troot than oany ye can see even at that fish ferm at Tauschentuch. Pit me doon, fur Goad's sake!" Can ye no' hear ma hair tearin' oot at the rits?"

"Well, let that be a lesson tae ye tae be polite tae yer superiors, ye snivellin' wee whelp ye," rasped Canny as he towered over him.

"Aye, an' tae get yer hair scythed doon!" whooped Billy Howker, who was just thinking that after the disastrous meal the social was really beginning to warm up to its usual white-heat atmosphere. This was the stuff of which Doonieburnie gatherings were made. "C'moan, Canny, here's yer prize!"

Another parcel, but this time of quite a different shape, about 12 inches by

9 inches. Canny wondered what on earth it could contain but, on reflection, he smacked his lips in gleeful anticipation. Perhaps a complete fly-tying outfit with the latest natty type of vice and including rare and much sought-after feathers, or a lightweight fishing coat to make up for the mistake Seamus had made the year before, or perhaps a huge box of minnows, enough to keep him going for a lifetime? With trembling fingers, which seemed as long as the parcel was broad, he tugged impatiently at the knots till they parted under broken fingernails. The paper was thrown aside to reveal a shining new creel, the smallest he - or anyone present - had ever seen.

"Ye glaikit bloody idiot. Ye've din it again! Last year a fishin' coat that wiz hardly big enough fur ma three-year auld bairn, this year a basket that's too wee even tae cairry ma piece! Hoo dae ye manage it?" And, quickly throwing the lid open, Canny turned the creel upside down and rammed it tightly over Seamus' head, ears and all, and, just to help it on its way and to make sure it stayed on for a bit, he banged it home with a blow from an irately clenched fist. Then he walloped it a thumping clout with the largest remaining part of the wading-stick, just to confirm that it would go no further. Seamus cried out in agony, the mental pain of this latest humiliation being almost as great as the physical, but eventually, with some help and a great deal of force and difficulty, he managed to extricate himself from his willowy cage. But some of its bars had been broken, which served to improve neither his physiognomy nor his complexion. Nor his composure for that matter.

However, Seamus had one great asset in that he always came bouncing back like a rubber ball. As authoritatively as ever, he called for attention:

"The special prize fur the most sportin' fisher amangst us hiz been won by a very courageous man fur jumpin' intae the Pauchle when it wiz in spate in richt cauld weather fur tae rescue Spud McDougall's big dug when it fell in. Well din, Dunky Todd!"

"Baloney!" roared Lochie Laidlaw, "A wiz fishin' next tae him. It wiz *him* that fell in an' it wiz the dug that jumped in an' poo'd him oot. It wiz starvin' o' hunger an' it thocht he wid mebbe gie it a bit o' his piece."

"That's no true," retaliated Dunky, "an' A can prove it because the dug had stole ma piece oot o' ma creel before that an' swallowed it a'."

"An' hoo dae ye prove that?"

"Noo, noo, nae mair o' that kind o' stuff, if ye please," came Seamus' highly original reply. "We must a' be as unselfish as Dunky when he jumped in tae save the dug."

"He widnae jump in tae save himsel'," retorted Lochie, whose grandfather, rumour had it, was of Irish stock.

"A' richt, a' richt, noo wull Mr. Todd please step forward tae get his weel-deserved prize!"

Tales of Fishing and Fishermen

Dunky hobbled out, clutching the leg which, he swore, was now riddled with rheumatism in consequence of the daring rescue he was supposed to have effected.

Again, it was a smallish box. And it was soon shown to contain a battery bicycle lamp. Loud guffaws resounded throughout the hall.

"Whit ye a' laughin' at?" yelled Seamus, embarrassed for the umpteenth time that evening and beginning to wonder if it was all worth it. "That's a very sensible prize, A ken fine Dunky disnae huv' a bike since the nicht he melted yon balloon wi' his whusky fumes efter he drove it through the butcher's windy an' got pit off the road. It's fur pittin' roond his waist when he's fishin' at nicht. It keeps yer haunds free!"

"We ken ye ken Dunky disnae huv' a bike but we ken tae whit he'll dae wi' that - dae ye no' ken tae?" bellowed Trabbie Tulloch, master as he was of an economic, fundamental English.

"Whit ye mean?"

"Dae ye no' ken? He'll walk doon through the shallow water in the dark wi' that lamp in yin haund an a pitchfork in the ither! He'll clean the place oot!"

Dunky turned on his adversary:

"Ye wid huv' mair tae worry aboot than that, ye black evil-minded bugger, if A hud a pitchfork here the noo fur if A hud A wid ram it richt up yer . . ." He just stopped on the brink, unusual for him.

"Noo, noo, Dunky," warned Seamus, "nane o' that kind o' language here. Mind this is a geentilmen's gatherin' and there are ladies present and you're supposed tae be a sportsman, Dunky, an example tae us a' an' above that kind o' talk. Dae ye no' like yer lamp?"

"It'll come in haundy, A suppose."

"Ungratefu' wee bugg . . ."

"Noo, noo, Seamus," shrieked Dunky, "mind whit ye jist said. Nane o' that language here. There's geentilmen an' ladies present."

Seamus reddened and felt annoyed he had let himself down in front of those he felt he had a duty to lead and instruct, not just in matters piscatorial, but moral as well.

"Sorry," he muttered, "but A'm gettin' a bit tired o' no' gettin' due recugnishun fur a' the hard graft A dae fur ye a'. Never mind, we've a' got a burden tae cairry an' youse yins seems tae be mine. Noo we'll a' hae a guid dance. But jist mind folks, we are no' in oor auld hall wi' yon crowd o' pail-bashers that ca' themselves the Doonieburnie Quarryblasters. We are in a posh hotel wi' its ain res...resident orch...orchist...orchister whit plays soft, soothin' music an' whaur a' the customers is toffs an' A wid jist remind ye tae dance nice an' sedate like an no' tae rattle the flairboards or huv' the plester fa'in doon off the ceilin' like ye usually dae. Fur anither thing, there's that big fancy chandaleer hingin' abune oor heids an' the dance flair is richt ow'er the top o' it an if it comes doon wi' a' the bangin' an' jumpin' an bashin' aboot, they'll mebbe no' let us come back next year."

"Is it a' richt if we draw braith when we're dancin', Seamus? Or dae we huv' tae wait till ye tell us?" quipped Billy Howker.

"Nae sarcastasm, please."

"But wha the hell wants tae come back here next year oanyway?" queried Sam McKendrick. "It micht be braw an' posh an' a' that but thae yins here dinnae ken nothin' aboot guid grub. A wid raither we wiz oan oor ain midden an' A wid raither huv' auld Skinty McGuffity's haggis an' neeps than a' the pigs' broke ye get here. We've been swicked. A think when we gaun up thae stairs we should bring the place doon, this chandaleer an' a' an' let thae smairt froggies see we're no' as daft as some o' us look - masel' excluded like."

"Weel, A never thocht ye wid ever admit it!" It was Billy Howker again, a Doonieburnian who was anything but slow to seize upon a play of words and to turn it round to suit him.

But Sam's suggestion met with roars of agreement and Seamus, eager to quell a situation which looked like developing into open rebellion, uttered another silent prayer and ushered those nearest him out of the dining-room and up to the magnificent ballroom where an immaculately-clad six-piece orchestra awaited their pleasure - or so they thought.

As Big Teenie, whose favourite number was the Doonieburnie Clog Dance, just couldn't wait to start swinging those mighty limbs and stamping those mighty feet, she grabbed Shugh Tarff by one ear - his whole one, he had lost most of the other when bitten by one of his ferrets - and ordered:

"C'moan. Ye're dancin'!"

"Aw, naw, A cannae, Teenie, A've a sair elba'."

"A sair elba'? Whit's yer elba got tae dae wi' it? Folk usually jig wi' thur feet, dae they no'? Are you jist tryin' tae insult me, yu fat slug?"

"Naw, naw, Teenie, ye ken fine A like dancin' wi' ye."

"Richt! C'moan an' see if we can git that chandaleer doon - it micht land oan top o' that manager's big bald heid if he's still doon there."

But the music offered wasn't nearly wild or rowdy enough to please her, so she stamped up to the orchestra and bawled in a voice that drowned their efforts completely:

"Whit ye think we're here fur, a burial? Fur Goad's sake pit some zip an' blast intae it afore we a' fa' asleep, wull ye no'? D'ye no' ken tunes like the Doonieburnie Dandies nur the Clug Dance?"

The pianist, to whom she addressed her polite oration looked blank, and it

Tales of Fishing and Fishermen

was difficult to tell whether the cause of his predicament was the language barrier or simply his inability to comply. He shook his head dolefully, marvelling at the diversity of social settings you could encounter in the same small district. A few evenings before he and his band had supplied the music for the twenty-first Birthday Party of Lady Petunia Prendergast-Smythe and her sophisticated entourage over at Castle Corrach in the next glen. One minute you were riding high on the crest of a beautiful wave, the next you were dumped down amongst the rubbish brought in by the tide.

"Weel, play some Heilan' stuff then!"

The pianist extricated himself from these sad ruminations and managed a sickly smile, as if in approval of her undoubted wit but then, noticing the aggressive glint in Teenie's eye and her colossal dimensions, he decided it wiser policy to take her request at face value. He had a quick word with his colleagues and within seconds the moonlight serenata which had earned the large lady's displeasure was replaced by an eightsome reel, the only music of this kind with which the band was familiar.

"Right Shughie, ma braw pairtner, c'moan. Intae that set!"

Shugh was dragged into the group, very much against his will as he had been involved with the Amazon in eightsome reels before and had seldom come out unscathed, but he knew only too well that a much more dire fate awaited him if he tried to make his escape. The men were put into the arena first, sexual discrimination having been a non-starter in Doonieburnie since time immemorial. The hardy independent females it bred would have had it no other way and with the dynamic firefly Lizzie Glen, the other lady with whom Shugh was concerned, he was whizzed from Teenie to Lizzie and from Lizzie to Teenie at such a tempo that he was convinced he had gone into orbit. Dizzy and exhausted, he yelled for mercy and the final crunch came when wee Lizzie, really warming to the fray, hauled him back by his new three-inch broad harvest-type braces, then heaved him forward, letting the elastic stretch to about 3 ft. before releasing her grip. Shugh shot forward plumb on target, which was, of course, the prancing Teenie. As far as the latter was concerned, the sensation was no more noticeable than that which might be felt by a mountain hit by a pebble. For Shughie, however, it was a case of the pebble being hit by the mountain. He was propelled towards the irresistible force Teenie like an arrow from a bow and collapsed in an inert heap at his partner's feet. He was shovelled into a corner, discarded like some piece of equipment which could no longer serve any useful purpose, while Mistress McTavish tried in vain to get a replacement, the spare men having made themselves scarce and utterly inaccessible. And even she drew the line at entering about the only remaining sanctuary that could legally be labelled " Men Only."

Another Night to Remember

By the early hours, even the normally tireless Doonieburnians had had enough, and the motor and tractor cavalcade that wended its way down the Doonie was much more subdued, like the river itself, which had fallen a few feet and again reflected the mood of those who loved it as they loved their peat-filled hearths at eventide, those simple sons of a Highland glen who, perhaps as a safety-valve to their hard daily grind, let themselves go once a year, tempestuous as the roaring flood, to drift back, like it, to quietness and placidity.

Piscatorial bliss?

It WAS one late spring evening that my wife popped a question, the full significance of which I was to realise before the season was much older:

"It's the end of April now. I suppose that means you'll soon be off on safari to the river every evening?"

It was the type of question we men hate, the one that has its origins in women's magazines with all their cosy talk about togetherness and romantic companionship for those who have left the first years of matrimonial bliss far behind them. It was the type of question which always lights a little red flame - with a keg of gunpowder right beside it. As with most men in a similar position, my problem was how to smother the flame before the explosion occurred.

"Well, you know dear, I've worked pretty hard throughout the winter - lot of overtime, not much relaxation. And fishing does me good, you know. It peps me up again."

"And what do I get to pep me up? What fun do I have? Cook, wash up, clean up, mop up, shop, knit, darn - does it never occur to you that I might need a change too?"

"Well," I said defensively, "you have your coffee mornings and Women's Guild and..."

"Coffee mornings? Once a month! Women's Guild - the ultimate in excitement? No, Peter, you'll have to do better than that!"

"All right, what d'you want me to do? Sell my tackle and sit here every night discussing Mrs. What's-her-name's latest hat?"

"No, I've decided that if you are so keen on fishing there must be something in it, so I'm going to take it up myself. After all, Women's Lib. and all that. A woman should be able to participate in the same sports as men - and some *do* fish, don't they? Mrs. Waddel says her husband will let me fish for trout."

You could have knocked me over with a wren's hackle. Mrs. Waddel was the wife of the farmer who had trout rights on the stretch I fished for salmon. The conspiracies that are concocted by women over endless cups of coffee! However, I suppose it could have been worse - at least I was going to the river.

It was a fine May evening when I had the unusual experience of setting off for the water with my wife in the passenger seat. I felt somewhat apprehensive and gone was that feeling of freedom, of escape from domestic stresses which, no matter how trivial, are not conducive to recuperation after the daily grind.

I had to assemble her tackle, of course. I gave her an old 8 ft. built-cane I never used, and a reel which sounded as if it was afflicted with chronic bronchitis. Then I tied on a cast.

"Why do I have only one small fly and you have two big ones?"

"Because, my dear, it is better that a beginner should fish a small single for trout. Less chance of tangles and more chance of a take."

"You sure it doesn't give me just once chance to your two of catching a fish?"

How could you answer a beginner with reasoning like that?

I prodded her gently into a shallow flat where, even in her gumboots, she could wade well away from the bank and the overhanging branches.

"Now try to cast across to where the breeze is rippling the surface." I knew small trout usually lay there.

I said I would go above her and try the narrow, rocky stream which usually held a salmon or two.

"Why are you going away up there and leaving me here all on my own? Are there more fish up there?"

I considered tightly closed lips to be the most discreet answer to that one, but I had hardly started to cast when she came up and walked in a couple of yards ahead of me.

"It's nice to fish together," she said, smiling benignly.

After being obliged to cease operations to extract the little Spider from her jacket, then from her hat, then to disentangle it from all round the top-piece of her rod, I thought I had finally got her settled. But it was not to be.

"Peter, this fly's no use. I want to try a worm!"

So as not to expend more energy in pointless argument, I waded ashore, changed her cast and handed her the tin of brandlings.

"Pick a nice lively one," I said.

"What do you mean? You surely don't expect me to touch one of those things? Pooh! Next time I'll bring my scent spray and give them a squirt!"

Next time, she had said. Hell!

The parr were voracious and after about half-an-hour I was exhausted by the continual efforts I had to make to unhook the little fish and to replace her bait. Then, when she jerked out an eel which had wound itself into a slimy ball and come swinging in to brush against her soft and still dimpled cheek, her screams were so strident that dozens of rooks rose from the treetops in sheer panic, adding their own none too musical contribution to vie, as it were, with Dorothy's. However, once I had pacified her - thanks mainly to a small box of her favourite milk chocolates as I had foreseen such an emergency - I told her to sit on the bank for a spell while I had a serious go in the stream. She sat down on my coat and renewed her lipstick before tackling her coffee creams and caramel cups.

A salmon - it must have been the blindest, deafest, most imperturbable and most stupid salmon that ever existed - actually took me. Dorothy came running.

"Bring it in, bring it in!"

"I can't bring it in. It's too heavy and strong. I'll have to tire it out first.

Tales of Fishing and Fishermen

Bring the big net, dear, and lay it down there on the gravel!"

"No, let me net it Peter. I can do it! Oh, please!"

Dorothy stood right beside me, somewhat cramping my style. Togetherness again, I suppose.

As the far from spent salmon came close in, she lunged at it, bringing the net down almost vertically.

"You're not catching butterflies!" I yelled. "Take it easy!"

She missed, of course - entirely, thank heaven - but the impetus of her swing pitched her headfirst into the water. I grabbed her with one hand while I tried to keep control of the panicking salmon - who could blame it? - which had now fled at full speed, plus a bit more, to get away from this female demon who had tried to batter it into the bed of the river.

"Never mind the fish! What about me?" she shrieked from lipstick-smeared lips and between splutters as the water ran down her face. "Just think of my hair! And I'm going to Jean's in the morning!"

I tried to keep calm as, miraculously, the fish was still on.

"Just two minutes, dear. This salmon has been subjected to such a trauma that it's nearly spent already. Just stand there quietly and I'll bring him in. Please don't move!"

"Don't move? Do you want me to catch my death of cold? Oh, how could you?"

I retrieved the net and slowly coaxed him in again. But he was still not beaten and when his eye caught this peculiar man and wife team he summoned up all his remaining strength and shot between Dorothy's legs before turning sharp back outstream.

My beloved wife was again pitched full force into the pool - on her back for a change. And this time she was so distressed that I had to put down my rod and pull her out. For a few brief moments words failed her and I thanked the gods for this thoughtful intervention on their part. Then I ran to pick up the rod.

"Oh, never mind the blessed thing! What about me, you chauvinistic boar?" (Dorothy had a penchant for playing around with set expressions). "It's just as I thought - you think more of fish than you do of your wife. I refuse to come back here with you. Never again, never! You can come on your own!"

I reeled in a slack line, but derived more than a crumb of comfort from the fact that I knew there would be no repeat of such a matrimonial cum piscatorial fiasco! There were places for "togetherness" and a salmon river certainly wasn't one of them!

Set a Poacher . . .

"DOCKIE" DUNCAN was one of those law-flouting individuals who will stop at nothing as far as poaching is concerned. The activity was not only a means of supplementing in more than handsome fashion the allowance he drew from Social Security, but was, as is so often the case, a way of life which seemed to fulfil some insatiable urge to seize what belonged to others and to turn it to financial gain. Perhaps in his case this attitude had stemmed from the teachings of his father who, even more illiterate than his son, had nevertheless been perspicacious enough to form a fairly accurate picture of the world around him and articulate enough to preach to his already wayward offspring the rank injustice of the social order, whose basic rule seemed to be that some would have and others would not, and that the former would leave no stone unturned to ensure that things remained that way. An over-simplification of the facts, of course, but it meant that Dockie, like his father before him, derived intense satisfaction from taking from those who seemed to have a superfluity of all the material belongings and amenities and pleasures which were traditionally denied to lesser mortals like himself.

Poaching for Dockie was an all-embracing, ruthless affair and no living creature of any culinary worth was safe from his marauding hands. Deer, pheasants, partridges, grouse, pigeons, hares, rabbits and fish were all considered by him to be God's gifts to man, to all men, and were meant to be there for the taking. So everything edible that ran or flew or crawled or swam was in danger when Dockie was around, which is synonymous with saying that they were under almost perpetual threat of attack. Salmon and sea trout in particular, because of their high market value and the ease of disposal, had to endure the brunt of his attentions from early spring until autumn, at a time when the deer and feathered game were out of condition, worth less and difficult to sell to the more principled dealers and hoteliers.

As with many like characters, scruples did not enter into it. Whereas some poachers, even the hardened variety, still retained a modicum of compassion for the prey they hunted and would have shied away from catching pheasants by placing a long nylon line with worm-baited hooks along the drills of a turnip field, or from having deer break their legs on falling into a pit dug in the forest, where they would lie squirming in agony sometimes for hours, Dockie felt no remorse whatsoever. The validity of any method he employed was measured only in terms of its practicability and its efficacy and he knew enough about the ways of this world to remind his horrified critics that far more dastardly crimes were committed every day by human against human and were merely shrugged off and tolerated, deeds which made his own misdemeanours pale into such insignificance as to be almost

Tales of Fishing and Fishermen

unworthy of mention. And even his most severe censors had to admit he had a point. Except, they would add, using that pathetic and time-worn cliché: "Two wrongs don't make a right."

It follows that Dockie was a perpetual torment to the authorities whose duty it was to uphold law and order. Elusive and cunning as he was nimble and silent, he glided about like one of the young deer he stalked in winter, apparently disappearing into thin air. Perhaps by studying the habits of the creatures he hunted he had learned much about the methods they themselves used to thwart their pursuers and on the few occasions when he had been cornered and caught, nothing was ever found on his person to incriminate him. One moment he might be loaded down with newly-caught game, the next he was as clean as a whistle. So, thorn as he was in the flesh of bailiffs, keepers and police, he was also something of a living legend throughout the neighbourhood, and there were few people, even those who tangled with him in his professional capacity, who did not have at least a sneaking regard for his knowledge and his ability and the downright originality of some of his ploys. Further, in an area where salmon poaching in particular was far from being a crime of low incidence and could boast more than the odd expert, he was regarded as a giant among dwarfs, and many skilled practitioners would willingly have sat at his feet.

Tam Urquhart, the head gillie and Watcher on one of Dockie's favourite hunting grounds, the River Donaig, was his sworn, inveterate enemy. In fact at times he was almost driven to distraction by the will o' the wisp Dockie, who went so far as to taunt him each time they met in the village inn - which was anything but a rare occurrence.

"Ach, Tam man, A hear there's a lot o' fush jist come up an' that the Cherry Tree is lyin' fu'. It'll no be fu' the morn'!" Dockie had always "heard about" the fish - in which case he must have frequently indulged in talking to himself. Moreover, he was adept at this kind of teasing, but was always careful enough not to admit any villainy outright and to ensure that what he said could have an alternative meaning.

The super-poacher would be annoyingly right because by "the morn'" the salmon would have moved up into other pools of the beat and a fair proportion of them removed therefrom. Dockie seemed to sense just how far the fish would travel in a given time under certain conditions of temperature and water level.

Tam would answer the veiled challenge with something like: "A'll git ye yet, Dockie. A'll git ye, even if it's wi' ma last breath." And Dockie would retort: "Noo, Tammy man, that widnae dae ye much guid, nur me neither. A wid hae tae gaun an' tell the polis whaur ye were lyin' because A wid hiv' enough tae cairry hame withoot huvin' tae sling a fat puddin' like you ower ma back."

The habitués of the Red Deer enjoyed the banter although it was not always welcomed by poor Tam, whose repertoire did not match Dockie's. He invariably felt he was something of a laughing stock and did not take too kindly to the idea of being looked upon as a source of free and regular entertainment. But no other pub was within range of his decrepit old bike and, therefore, nowhere else where he could partake of his regular intake of Mountain Tarn.

One July morning at day-break, when the river was low but contained a good stock of fish which had come in on a previous flood, Tam, surveying part of the beat with binoculars from a vantage point in an elevated gap amongst the trees, spied a familiar-looking figure bent over the rocks jutting out of the stream at the head of The Tunnel.

"Got ye this time, ye slippery divil!" he muttered revengefully.

Tam had served for some time as a sort of Highland cowboy with the herds in the Great Glen and the lasso that was sent out with unerring aim a few minutes later landed squarely round Dockie's wiry shoulders, pulling him back off the rock and into the river. This was Tam's latest brilliant idea to catch his poacher unawares, so that he would then have no time to dispose of the incriminating equipment undoubtedly hanging round his neck. He was then hauled violently ashore.

Dockie belched out about a gallon of cold, peaty water, but, his reactions as lightning as ever, he managed to spew it accurately all over Tam's grisly countenance. Then, when both men had finally spluttered and coughed themselves back to something approaching normality, Dockie yelled:

"Whit's the game? Whit ye think ye're tryin' tae dae? A could huv' got drooned, ye murderous tyke, ye."

Tam was somewhat taken aback, not by Dockie's vehement outburst, to which type of challenge he was long accustomed, but by the fact that he could see no cleek or snare accompanying the glass-bottomed can suspended from his arch-enemy's neck. Actually, the latter, conditioned as he was to swift reaction, had had the presence of mind to drop his length of wire when he was so unceremoniously snatched from his mid-river stance. Even so, Tam reckoned that the "peerin' can", as Dockie called his poaching aid, would be evidence enough to get his adversary into a tighter spot than he had so far managed to manipulate him:

"Whit were ye daein' oot there? Whit's that beer can daein' roon' yer neck? Ye'll be tellin' me next you've started cairryin' yer booze aboot like a St. Bernard dug!"

"Haw, haw, ye're a richt comedian, richt enough, Tam. Ye should be on the television wi' a' thae ither goats. Ye wid jist need tae stand an' look an' folk wid burst thursels. Ye wid be made, man. An' that wid be easier than trampin' up an' doon a river a' day an' nicht an' catchin' naebody. Wull A

Tales of Fishing and Fishermen

write tae the high heid yins an' tell them whit they're missin'?"

"Dinnae try tae change the subject. Gie's that can!"

Dockie handed it over almost angelically, bowing politely, with the words: "A only got six."

"Six? Ye admit ye got six salmon?"

"Wha mentioned salmon? Mister Urquhart, sur, A huv' been after mussels an' A got six."

"Mussels? Mussels?"

"Aye, A look through the glass at the bottom o' the can an' a can see the mussels on the bottom o' the river."

"An' whit may A ask, whit dae ye dae wi' mussels? A'm jist kinda curious like, ye ken."

"Hivens, Tam, ye're an awfu' ignorant man. D'ye no ken they often huv' perrils in them?"

"Per-rils? Whit dae ye dae wi' them, sook them?"

"A said per-rils, no pandrops."

"Oh, ye mean thae dear things posh women huv' hingin' frae thur lugs or on a rope roond thur necks?"

"Aye, look!"

Dockie took out one of the mussels from the pouch he wore permanently round his waist to deal with just such a contingency, although one has to admit it had other uses, being a handy receptacle for things such as pheasants' eggs and the roe he nimbly stripped from gravid autumn salmon and sold at a high price to trout fishers from the Central Belt. Using his knife, he prized open three of the mussels before he found the one he wanted. It contained a white plastic pearl he had taken from an old Woolworth's necklace he had found hanging from a neighbour's dustbin.

"See, Tammy son, A'm in luck. This per-ril wull get me aboot fifteen quid when A tak' ma year's catch tae Glesca in the backend."

"Awa' ye bletherin' dumb-bell. Ye think A'm as green as a hazel stick?"

"Ye're as green as a newborn grasshopper wi' nae heid. An' aboot as braw, tae. Bit A'm tellin' ye, man. Hoo dae ye think A got ma new telly? An' ma greenhoose an' ma new bunnet?" The first two items had actually come from the bumper haul of salmon he had taken the previous season, together with what he had fiddled from the Social Security, and the third had been nonchalantly exchanged for his own indescribably unbecoming head-gear from a large store during a visit to Glasgow.

But Tam, who was not unknown for his slightly gullible attitude when he heard things he liked to hear, had had his interest aroused:

"Ye mean ye git thae per-rils oot o' thae mussel things that ye git oot o' the river? Bit A've never seen thae shelly things before!"

"There's an awfu' lot o' things ye've never seen before! Bit that's because they look like stanes an' ye need a glass like mine tae pick them oot. Mind ye, they huvnae a' got per-rils in them, bit a fair wheen o' them huv'. Ye've jist tae keep tryin'. Ye can open a hunder o' them an' git nothin' an' then the next five or six a' huv' per-rils in them, an' before ye ken whaur ye are ye're awa buyin' yersel' a new pair o' galasses - A mean a new bike or somethin'."

It was well known in the neighbourhood that mentioning braces to Tammy was like holding a bright red rag to an already enraged bull. This apparently neurotic aversion of Tam's to an innocent and effective device for holding up one's breeches had its origins in the day he had climbed a silver birch to observe Dockie as the latter was, in turn, observing some leaping salmon. Unfortunately, a branch had snapped and he had been left suspended until the buttons on his moleskins had finally succumbed and he'd become immersed in a rather smelly peat bog. Dockie, of course, had always derived great pleasure from the incident and, fond as he was of seeing his protagonist wriggle, he introduced the word into his conversations with Tam at every available opportunity.

"Are they every place in the river?" queried the gillie.

"No, the best place is the flat below the Craw's nest." It almost goes without saying that the stretch of water mentioned wasn't an ideal spot for salmon poaching.

Dockie drew profit from this latest confrontation on three accounts. He had extricated himself successfully from an awkward situation; he knew Tam would now spend a good deal of time on the flat until he found out the truth or got fed up with his lack of success, which would give Dockie more room for manoeuvre at a time when the grilse were shoaling upstream; and, lastly, he always enjoyed coming out top in any challenge from a river official, especially if the man in question was Tam Urquhart.

Such tricks were common over the years and many were the dodges conjured up by pursuer and pursued, but eventually when Tam, a few years senior to Dockie in age, became somewhat long in the tooth and decided to call it a day, Dockie too was finding himself less and less able to cope with the strength-sapping and often dangerous demands of his chosen profession. As the bartender at the inn remarked, even a deer can muster only a gentle trot eventually.

So you could have knocked Dockie over with a No. 10 Blue Dun when, one April morning, he was summoned before the Donaig's proprietor, Colonel Beck:

"Well now Duncan," began the Colonel, "tell me, I reckon you know my river like the palm of your hand?" He noted that the palm of Dockie's hand

Tales of Fishing and Fishermen

was like a piece of dirty, gnarled bark but, he reflected, that did nothing to weaken the validity of the simile.

Dockie was at once on the *qui-vive*, uncertain of where this opening remark was leading.

"Well, ower the years A've had the odd dander along it, ye ken."

"You know the best lies on every size of water, don't you?"

"Well, ye ken, A've aye watched the salmon jumpin' an' A've aye been interested in thae fishes' habits. A think A'm a bit o' a conversationist."

"A conservationist?" The Colonel smiled, not over the error of vocabulary but at the undisguised hypocrisy of the man.

"I think we might say your interest in salmon has extended far beyond their various idiosyncrasies, however?"

"A huvnae heard o' that pool before. Whaur is it?"

"No, what I am saying Duncan, is that you are intimate with the fish movement in the river and your knowledge would be a definite asset when I start letting the beat out to visitors next week. There is no better advertisement than having the services of someone who knows where most salmon are likely to be lying at any given moment."

"So whit are ye gettin' at? Ye want me tae clean a' the fush oot before thae visitors can get at them?"

"No, no, Duncan! Now listen carefully. I am prepared to take an unprecedented step - I had a reputation for doing this in North Africa you know, as our old friend Rommel knew to his cost. I am prepared to pay you a handsome wage if you keep your eye on the water and give all the advice you can to our visitors, to see that they catch salmon and want to come back. What's more - and this is equally important - I hear from a reliable source that gangs of poachers are gradually extending their sphere of activities northwards to include this area, and I need someone.... someone, who.... is familiar with their nefarious ways and can deter them from visiting my beat."

Dockie gulped in sheer disbelief.

"Ye mean A've tae be a poacher-catcher? Me? Me on the side o' the polis? Whit a laugh! A wid never live it doon. A wid never be able tae show ma face in the Red Deer again. A wid be oostersized!"

"Duncan, a guaranteed £55 per week, plus generous tips no doubt, plus that attractive little cottage by the bridge, no more rising in the middle of the night. . . ."

"Ye'd better step back oot o' the road if ye dinnae want tae get yer feet wet fur the water's beginnin' tae rin doon ma chin! Ach man, hoo can A refuse a - whit dae ye ca' it - a sinycoor like that! Ye're on!"

"Fine! Fine! But I must stipulate one essential condition, Duncan - much as you may be tempted, you are to leave the salmon well alone. Promise?"

"Ach man, A've felt fur a while noo that A'm gettin' too doddery fur that sort o' thing onyway. A'm no as sure-fitted as A wiz. Jist the ither day when A wiz cleekin' a fush A slipped an' let him tak' the haundle richt oot o' ma haund - an A fell an' got ma dood...A mean ma tentacles jammed between twa rocks an' A huvnae been the same since. So maybe this job's come at the richt time."

"Fine, Duncan, fine. Can you start right away?"

"No' till Monday. The morn A've tae gaun tae Glesca wi' a big bag o'....o' tatties fur ma sister." And he added hastily: "Tatties dinnae grow very well in the Gorbals, ye ken."

Colonel Beck did not bother to point out that the transportation of a bag of potatoes to Glasgow was economic foolishness, as several bags could have been bought in that city for the fare alone, but decided not to pursue the subject. After all, this would be the last consignment of salmon which Dockie, after an illustrious career in the field, would deliver to one of his contacts, and he might as well be allowed to make the most of it before he donned respectable social garb and, for the first time in his life, was on the side of the toffs and the capitalists he had always professed to abhor.

Ricochet

So COMMON were the shoddy tactics in operation at the Annual Competition of the Rauchletoggie Angling Club that the Committee, determined to clean up what for years on end had been nothing short of a complete and utter farce, decreed that the competition would henceforth be held in daylight instead of during the hours of darkness. But as the Toggie was invariably low in July it was also decided that the event would take place during the first flood of the month, from 8 am to 6 pm. Entrants were, therefore, advised to have all their tackle ready as soon as the rains came and a flood was obviously in the offing. Any legal method would be permissible. Unfortunately, a lot of the trouble usually stemmed from the fact that some of them had little idea of what 'legal' methods were - and didn't bother too much to find out. And those who did know, would not be slow to devise new and ingenious tricks to replace those which they would have used so effectively under cover of darkness. So the organisers weren't so naïve as to believe that the new arrangements would cancel out entirely all the unacceptable joukery-pawkery which had characterised previous tournaments. Even so, they still cherished the hope that participants, knowing their actions could now be observed, would be deterred from succumbing to at least the most blatant malpractices. Well, no one could blame them for hoping.

Fred Robb expressed vocal pleasure on drawing the top half of The Stewpot. His great rival of long standing, Bert McGurk, drew the bottom half of the same pool.

Fred made no secret of the fact that he was going to try "meat balls" because "the troots wull be fair burstin' wi' a' the worms an' maggots that huve came doon the last hoor or twa". So, he argued, a novel change of menu was on the cards.

"Meat balls? Balls tae you tae!" exclaimed Bert. "Hoo the hell dae ye expect troots tae tak' meat balls? Whit are ye gie'n' them fur a puddin'? Tapioca?"

The meat balls were, in fact, spheres of salmon roe, about half-an-inch in diameter, which Fred had steeped overnight in gravy. This, he figured, would help to disguise the "bait" and to kill the distinctive smell until the ball hit the water and the gravy was washed off - which, in his opinion, was all that was required for his ruse to remain undetected. It was a real stroke of genius on which he congratulated himself time and time again. Fishing in daylight would have no disadvantages as far as he was concerned.

And in fact it wasn't long before the trout began to savage the forbidden offering. And so large and succulent were the balls used that the scent drifted down the current to the attractive eddy where Bert was plying his rod, which

meant that the hitherto disinterested brownies. affected by the appetising flavour of the salmon eggs, now began to attack his worms ravenously. Fred saw him take nearly as many as himself, which annoyed him, all the more so because he knew the reason why. And Bert, too was annoyed, because he now suspected what Fred was using on his hook. He himself had deemed roe to be too risky and had been unable to think up any new ploy which might make for a heavier basket.

"Ye sure thae 'meat balls' are no awfu' red inside?" he teased.

"Aye, it's raw meat a' made them oot o'. A ran o'er a hedgehug wi' the tractor last nicht."

"Well," retorted Bert, "hoo come ye're catchin' troots wi' them? Troots never sees raw hedgehug's puddins."

"Naw," answered Fred, "an' they never sees fancy flees made oot o' feathers a' the colours o' the rainbow either, bit they still try tae ate them".

"Hoo dae *you* ken? Aw, c'moan, Fred. A' ken fine whit ye've got on yer hook."

"An' ye only ken because ye've been catchin' troots below me." answered Fred. "If A hudnae hud the toffee, ye wid huve got buggerall. So A think ye shid gie me hauf o' yer catch. An' A'm bein' generous at that!"

"You kiddin'?" exploded Bert. "Whit a bloody cheek! Ye cheat at the fishin' an' then want tae cheat mair by takin' some ither puir bugger's hard-earned troots. Nae winder yer second name's Robb!"

"Tell ye then, Bert, A'll gie ye twa quid fur the lot!"

"Twa quid? Fur echt braw fish weighin' aboot six pund? Awa' an..."

The conversation was interrupted momentarily while Fred dragged out a brownie which obviously scaled nearer 3 lb. than 2 lb. Bert now knew that, with his own substantial catch added to it, Fred would have an excellent chance of landing at least one of the subsidiary prizes, if not the first prize itself.

"Fower quid an' ye can huve them!" ventured Bert.

"Bollocks!" roared Fred. "Bit A'll split the difference!"

"Eh, a' richt. Bit A want 20 pence fur every ither troot A catch an' gie ye. Ur it's no oan!" demanded Bert.

"Greedy bugger. Bit A suppose so."

"Well, it's tae your benefit tae, isn't it? The mair troots ye huve, the better yer prize'll be. An' wi' a' this lot A hive here an' yer ain bagfu' there an' the ithers we'll catch ye'll huve a guid chance."

"A' richt. Here, tak' some o' ma toffee. Ye'll catch even mair. A'll git mair troot an' you'll git mair cash."

Bert had to admit this was a fair argument. It wasn't often you got a transaction which didn't produce a loser.

Tales of Fishing and Fishermen

At the end of the day, Bert had over £4 in his pocket and Fred had a creel bulging with brownies ranging from $1/2$ lb to 2 lb. 10oz. Weigh-in was scheduled for 7 pm, and Bert accompanied his confederate into a room bursting at the seams with competitors, all curious to know how everyone had fared. Bert was half-hoping to receive an extra cash payment from his accomplice if the latter succeeded in landing one of the premier awards, though he doubted it.

But the chief of the panel of three referees, no less a figure than William McCandless himself, the club secretary, a model of rectitude in the neighbourhood, a revered dignitary in all walks of social life, church elder, police judge, councillor - name it and, if it existed, he was it or had been it - spotted something small, squashed and pink-coloured adhering to one of the trout. His reaction was to prod an exploratory finger down some of the fish's throats and in no time at all, he had ejected on to the table enough salmon ova to fill half the trays in a good-sized hatchery.

William McCandless - a keen angler himself - drew himself up to his full height (which was considerable) and, sticking out his chest (which was not), he riveted steely grey eyes on Fred and pronounced in a voice which was pregnant with reproach:

"Fred Robb, I am ashamed of you. Not only have you cheated in the competition but, by stooping so low, you have brought disgrace on yourself, on our angling club and in fact on the entire community. You will no doubt be expelled when the committee meets to deal with your case. What is more, this is a criminal offence and you will be reported to the police immediately."

"A'll be reported tae the polis, ye say? Well, in that case Mr. McCandless, sur, ye can report me fur somethin' else while ye're at it. A theft! Hear me? Aye, a theft, because A stole that roe oot o' that auld shed ye huve at the bottom o' yer gairden. There's dizens an dizens o' jars o' it in there."

Remorse?

THEY USED TO SAY that when Big John Currie was not murdering fish he was murdering children and vice-versa. But this was a misleading and unfair criticism (in fact often pronounced in jocular rather than serious fashion) of the tall, strapping schoolmaster who had spent his entire career - he was now in his early fifties - trying to teach in what used to be and sometimes still is, one of those efficient, well-disciplined six-year schools situated in a smallish Scottish country town and catering for a large rural community. He certainly "murdered" his pupils in the sense that he stood for no nonsense and worked them till they were often mentally exhausted. Not for him the liberal ideas of many modern educationalists, whom he dismissed as nincompoops of the first order and their theories as so much undiluted balderdash. So it goes almost without saying that there was none of this "equal term" stuff between teacher and taught - in fact if any pupil had had the ill-considered audacity to address him in too familiar a manner, it would probably have been the last word he would have uttered for a long, long time, so great would have been the shock to his system.

Big John, basically full of good sense, could pardon slowness and stupidity, but not laziness or indifference, as he did not see why he should exert himself if the response was nil. So he was admired and liked both by those who were bright and industrious and by those who sincerely tried, but couldn't, and detested like the plague by the slothful.

So the best antidote to an entire class of bovine, unteachable fifteen-year olds, which he had to thole on three occasions each week, was the river and the peace of mind and body it had to offer.

There were three louts in particular, three unwashed, arrogant louts (though what they had to be arrogant about only God knew), perfect examples of the type who, a few years before, the State had said deserved and needed a further year of "education" - as if all they required to do was to sit down on a school bench and knowledge would come flowing in through the seat of their pants - who hated Big John with a hate which could only be described as vicious, perhaps even dangerous. They had subdued and at times terrorised nearly every other teacher in the school, but Big John remained an unconquerable bastion, and it narked.

With their simple monkey minds, they tried to concoct a plan which would avenge them for the mighty wallops that regularly sent them tottering after they had voiced an impertinence or committed some other offence more reminiscent of a farmyard than a classroom. "Stupo" McNeil thought they should waylay Big John one dark night and set about him with bicycle chains enhanced with wrappings of barbed wire. "Droopy" Sinclair was all for it, but the other member of the trio. "Stewie" Blunt, who was considered to

Tales of Fishing and Fishermen

have a glimmer of intelligence more than the others (although that was debatable) feared that they might come off worse in any physical confrontation with their powerfully-built tormentor. The odds, at three to one, were not good enough, and Stewie went on to suggest a plan where there was no danger of thumping retaliation and which, for him, was subtle in the extreme.

They knew Big John spent most summer nights on the river and that on Fridays he usually fished right through till the following dawn. So they would frighten the living daylights out of him. They would make him renounce his chief pleasure for ever. He would never fish at night again or even perhaps in daytime, so terrifying would be his memories of what would be his last night spent on the river bank. He might even be a changed man for the rest of their enforced attendance at school.

Big John noticed, and noted, their much less antagonistic attitude in class and suspected something was afoot. Meantime, the three of them had found out, as surreptitiously as was possible considering the limited mental faculties at their disposal, when and where their teacher habitually started operations with rod and line and, one Friday evening in mid-July, hid themselves in some neighbouring brushwood about an hour before dusk.

Their quarry arrived some thirty minutes later and slowly - because he was in no hurry - began to assemble his tackle. The trio, well concealed, watched him, their oafish countenances twisted into cruel, determined distortion.

Big John, a little puzzled by a faint but distinctive odour which he seemed to recognise as reminiscent of another milieu, reckoned that it was now dark enough, that the enchanting hour had come, and stepped quietly into the pool, making his reel sing as he stripped off line.

The three youths, crouching amongst the brooms, hadn't enough grey matter amongst them to realise that their ploy might be more effective if they waited until darkness had fully descended, when that complete and noisy silence, which can unnerve even the most realistic of men, had settled over the water and its surroundings. Perhaps they themselves felt somewhat uneasy on this alien soil, accustomed as they were to the bright lights of the café and its eternal ear-splitting juke-box.

So Big John had made hardly half-a-dozen casts when Droopy could contain himself no longer. Being the instigator of aggression always boosted his ego for the next six months, so he cupped his grubby hands to his rounded lips:

"Hwooo! Hwoooo! Hwooooo!"

Big John, who had spent literally hundreds of nights on dark rivers, was startled only in so far as he could not identify the sound. He knew intimately

Remorse?

the calls of the various species of owl - and this was not one of them. He was puzzled. Puzzled, but not alarmed.

"Hwoooooo!"

The sound might well have sent tremors up and down the spine of the habitual city-dweller in no way conversant with the nocturnal scene, but not in Big John's case. Then once more he detected that distinctive smell which was contaminating the breeze. There was only one place where he had experienced it before. Classroom 26. The nauseating odour of unclean flesh.

He decided to give the impression that he had fallen for their ruse. Stamping noisily ashore, he quickly dismantled his rod, picked up his creel and trotted off, making his simulated panic obvious by crashing through the long grass and bushes. Then he slowed his pace to give them time to follow, which they did. Their type was not very good at standing up to an attack but, by Jove, how they could give chase to those they deemed to be afraid.

Big John knew the terrain. And he knew they didn't. So he made for the open conduit running down from the piggery, a thin trickle of vile-smelling liquid bordered on each side with a good yard of the accumulated gunge of months, about a foot deep, soft as putty, almost impossible to detect in the dark. A quick glance behind him revealed the outlines of the figures following in hot pursuit.

He found the narrow plank without any appreciable halt in his pace, stepped nimbly over it and turned round the end of the dyke, where he kneeled on the short grass and peered back.

The trio arrived, now running as fast as their legs and lungs would let them, now convinced they had reduced the fugitive to a quivering jelly quite incapable of defending himself. They were already anticipating the pleasure of putting the boot in.

They plunged almost simultaneously into the stench-ridden goo and the momentum of their bodies propelled them forwards and downwards in beautiful belly-flops. Each purple face contacted the liquid dung with a resounding smack and went in a good three inches. And all three panting mouths were wide open. Ideal instruments of suction.

Big John smiled once more as he watched his would-be persecutors stumbling about in blind confusion, choking and spluttering, coughing and moaning ("Christ, whit a bloody taste!"), unable to orientate themselves, not even having the sense to make downhill towards the river and at least partly cleanse themselves. Finally, they wandered off, completely shattered both physically and emotionally. Poor souls, they could not commit even simple assault and make a job of it.

Big John went back to his fishing and, unmolested by man or beast, creeled a half-dozen handsome sea trout between then and dawn.

Tales of Fishing and Fishermen

Stupo, Droopy and Stewie, notorious truants, were absent from school during the whole of the following week, and when the attendance officer called at their respective houses he was surprised to find they were genuinely sick. The doctor had diagnosed some queer form of food poisoning, blaming it on some old mutton pies they had consumed at one of their homes early on that fateful Friday evening. When they eventually appeared in class, the venom in their faces was more apparent than ever. Well, thought Big John, if they want a personal vendetta, if they want all-out war, they can have it. And he was on his guard.

One night, about a fortnight later, not long after he had started fishing - again it was a Friday - the teacher noticed a fierce glow from the spot where he had left his car. Then came an explosion and an almighty fire.

By the time he got there, he was powerless to do anything but stand and watch. Soon only a charred hulk remained.

There was a further explosion when the temper, which up till now he had always managed to keep under strict control, swelled to the surface in unmitigated fury. Months of baiting on their part and the tension born of silent suffering on his, had finally brought about the situation he had always dreaded. His anger was still simmering dangerously on the Monday morning when he sent for them and questioned them right away about their whereabouts the preceding Friday. They were obviously cagey and perturbed, even scared. The simmer came back to the boil, for their attitude was proof enough and removed any lingering doubts he might have had. Leaving his belt in the drawer of his desk, he took each of them in turn into a remote bookstore and "sorted them out" in the old-fashioned way, accomplishing in a few seconds what the so-called Children's Panels and Juvenile Courts would have failed to achieve in a year, if ever.

During the afternoon a police inspector and a sergeant arrived to apprehend the trio for a robbery that had taken place in a neighbouring town late on the Friday evening. There was infallible proof that they were the culprits.

On hearing the news Big John, confused, adjourned to the Staff Common Room for a much-needed smoke. It was when he took out his packet that he suddenly remembered the lighted cigarette he had dropped when he had bent over to lift his creel from the back seat and, in his hurry to get from car to water, had forgotten to pick up.

Opportunity Knocks

GILLIE Angus Sloan, a knowledgeable, self-taught man, an avid reader of worthwhile literature and an exponent of a homespun philosophy which was brimful of practicability and good sense, had for years cherished a burning ambition - to have an angling book accepted and published. True, he had had occasional articles printed in sporting magazines, even a couple in a glossy, prestige monthly, but to be the author of an impressive volume with coloured plates of his own fly patterns and photographs of himself beside pools on his Laird's beat, with great fresh-caught salmon displayed in all their glory at his feet, and to lace his prose with thrilling anecdotes, couthy remarks and helpful hints - that became his supreme aspiration in life. After all, he did little but fish or look after fishing guests or tie flies to please the latters' every whim. And, having that Scottish love for words and the ability to set them down in a lively, punchy style, he had time to indulge in what others, occupying the same or similar stations in life as himself, considered flippant, even deserving of scorn, not at all in keeping with what was expected of an expert on *salmo salar* and the fine river which sheltered the fish in their teeming thousands. While Angus sat for hours battling with words, often fruitlessly, his peers would earn an extra pound or two giving instruction to would-be fly fishers and failed to understand that Angus' ambition had become an obsession, an all-embracing desire that could be assuaged only by its ultimate realisation.

Nevertheless, the gillie was adamant about one thing - the book had to be published on its merits, it had to be published because a publisher deemed it worthy of being published. He would have none of this pathetic business whereby you got your work in print by paying a firm an extortionate sum for a few dozen copies to hand out to your friends. That would have been an obscenity, since he was well aware that hardly a single book which appeared in this way was worthy of the paper used in its production.

So he got to work, engaging a first-class local photographer who made a magnificent job of the coloured-plates, producing superb pictures of a superb Highland river sweeping down in all its glory between banks of Scots pine and silver birch, of gillie Sloan standing in nonchalant fashion with his 14 ft. fly rod and the morning's catch spread out before him, or depicting him in action out in the water, shooting a long, perfect line across the Pheasant's Nest or the Brandy Bottle.

Angus wrote the script during one close season, editing and chiselling and revising and chiselling again till he believed the work to be a model of artistic perfection. Then he set about finding a publisher. But, what with rising costs of newsprint, spiralling wages and inflation, such gentlemen were going through difficult times and accepting only titles which were practically

certain to succeed. The first three rejected it - reluctantly they said, because it had much to recommend it, but they rejected it just the same.

Rather despairingly, he sent it to a fourth. Its receipt was acknowledged and the note, signed with a squiggle with the word "Editor" underneath, promised a decision as soon as possible. It all looked very impressive, even hopeful, and Angus somehow felt a little more confident.

Then, a few days later, he received an unexpected telephone call. "Editor here, Smythe and Grayson." The voice went on to say he was an enthusiastic angler himself and swore he would do his utmost to ensure publication at the next meeting of the committee whose function it was to come to a decision on the various manuscripts received, and with whom his word counted for much. He added, almost as a sort of oral postscript, that he would be coming north in the summer and that if the gillie could arrange some fishing for him on that delectable river so tantalising described in *King Salmon*, he would try to show his gratitude in a manner which the gillie would appreciate.

Angus suspected it was a bribe, camouflaged perhaps, but a bribe even so. But at the same time he was astute enough to realise that his caller must have rated the book highly, otherwise he would not have compromised himself in this manner.

After all, following three successive rejections, Angus was now quite desperate. He looked at the guest list for July and August, picking out the quietest week coinciding with the Laird's absence in London, and waited for the next call which had been arranged for a certain day in June - not without some trepidation, for he had never done anything of this nature before and although the Laird was a reasonable man, even at times a kindly man, he conferred few favours and expected absolute obedience and unfailing loyalty. Angus sweated a little when he recalled how a groom had been shown the Estate gates a year or two before when, without asking for permission, he had allowed one of his wee nieces to have a short canter on one of the prize ponies. Yet too much was at stake for him not to take the risk, and he made up his mind not to flinch when that telephone began to ring. And flinch he did not.

The Londoner duly arrived. Angus explained the awkwardness and even the danger of his position and issued strict instructions about where his guest had to fish - at the far downstream extremity, rarely visited by other guests because of its inconvenience rather than its unproductivity, for it was every bit as good as elsewhere. Angus, needless to say, did his best, mainly by enthusing about the large number of fish inhabiting the topmost pools, to keep the others well away from the intruder. Not that anyone was likely to wander off down to the danger zone, but he had to try to make sure that no one did.

Opportunity Knocks

The Londoner, who stayed at a local hotel, caught fish on each outing except one and was highly pleased. On his departure, he gave Angus to understand that he would get a letter very soon informing him his book was accepted for publication. And that if the gillie could arrange a similar holiday for him the following summer he would be more than delighted. Perhaps he had other volumes in mind?

Angus received the letter all right and it contained the news he expected and wanted. Several months later copies of the book, which sold well right from the outset, stood in a conspicuous position on his bookshelves, next to works such as *Animal Farm, The Rise and Fall of the Third Reich* and *H.M.S. Ulysses*. The Laird himself bought several copies, proud as he was of his gillie's literary prowess, and sent them to his fishing friends, of whom he had many.

For Angus there was just one question mark, something which even in the beginning gnawed at him from time to time. Would the book really have been published if the Editor hadn't been a keen fisher and he, Angus, hadn't accepted what had probably been a bribe? As time went on, he doubted it very much and every time he picked up a copy of *King Salmon* he felt more and more that he had cheated, that he had fallen victim, albeit to only a small degree, of the underhand dealings and corruption that he knew to be part and parcel of so many business transactions. His cake, which at first he had believed to be composed of such satisfying ingredients, gradually lost its sweet taste and became rather bitter. Eventually the mere sight of the book scunnered him, and he hid all his copies away in a cupboard. And he no longer derived pleasure from putting pen to paper.

A pity, because his book had been published on its merits alone. The man who had phoned him and come to fish was an editorial assistant, a keen angler and sharp-minded individual who knew everything that was going on and never missed the chance to exploit a situation and grab whatever he could.

It was the firm's expert panel of sports advisers who had recommended publication. The Editor hardly knew one end of a rod from the other.

The Invasion

SITTING one warm evening on the bridge over the Troochie Burn, Totty McShin was chatting with the old and craggy ex-postman, Gavie Sinclair, moaning about his inability to attract the huge trout of The Muckle Loch. He had tried every type of fly, including butterflies and dragonflies, as well as worms, maggots, grasshoppers, slugs, snails - practically every small creature that flew or crawled - everything. Or so he thought.

"Try a puddock!" advised old Gavie.

"A whit?"

"A puddock. A P-U-D-D-O-C-K. Ye ken whit a puddock is?"

"Aye, but..."

"But whit? Catch ane or twa puddocks, big, slimy, greasy yins, stick a big hook through a hint leg and git yersel' oot at the break o' day. Ye'll git bigger troots than ye've ever seen."

Totty always had a ready ear for advice, especially if it pertained to his first love, the water, and came from an experienced veteran like Gavie Sinclair, who in his day had had many a tense battle with the mighty ferox of the Western Highlands. And, questionable as this particular item of information sounded, Totty considered he had nothing to lose. In any case, it looked as if some new and original approach was needed.

However, frogs were not too easy to come by in the neighbourhood, mainly because of the dry weather, and he had to tramp a rough two miles to a hill pond to capture half-a-dozen. He felt his efforts well rewarded, however, when he at last managed to tempt a couple of the dour denizens of The Muckle. One, a bonnie, well-made fish, scaled 4lb; and the other, an ugly-looking bull, half of it head and with a kype like an old-fashioned tin-opener, weighed just over $5^1/2$ lb. But it was still a trout, and from now on he knew which bait to use.

He knew which bait to use and his success continued. But supplies were still difficult to obtain and too much tramping was involved, too much searching. Too much time was being spent hunting frogs instead of trout. He had to find a simpler way.

He found it.

That autumn the McShin garden, a good quarter-acre which was a tangle of dockens and clumps of nettles interspersed with sickly-looking cabbages and the wilting stalks of plants that had tried their honest best to be something or other, became, for the first time ever, the scene of a vast digging operation. Helped by one or two not too willing cronies (they were promised regular supplies of big trout for years to come), a massive hole was dug and lined with a sheet of polythene.

A foot of soil was shovelled back in and it and the surrounding edges planted thick with reeds of every description, procured from the bog pond. The hole was then filled with water and, after further expeditions into the hills, Totty was able to introduce prime stock in the shape of half-a-dozen mature "puddocks".

They seemed to accept their new surroundings as a home from home, and the following year the tadpoles appeared in shoals. Then, at the first glimpse of the leaping little frogs, Totty rubbed his hands together. His fishing was secure. The water level of The Muckle would drop by the time he had finished.

Not wishing to erode his future stock, however, and because old Gavie had said you needed big puddocks in any case, he continued to make his safaris to the bog - and to take more than the occasional heavy trout from the loch. He could hardly wait for the following season when he would have an endless and unrestricted supply of big, choice puddocks.

The frogs multiplied at a speed and in numbers beyond his wildest hopes. Then it started.

A particularly showery spell of weather seemed to give his precious stock a bout of wanderlust and he was warned of the first sign of trouble when his next-door neighbour, the massive and redoubtable Jessie Johnstone, came out to bring in some washing she considered would be just about right for ironing.

As she bent down to place a sheet in her basket, a big bull puddock, full of his own importance and his mouth dripping with froth, jumped a good foot into the air to startle her to such an extent that Jessie emitted a piercing scream and staggered back, fell over a rustic clothes pole and ended up on her back in her husband's bed of prize Sir Winston Churchills and President Herbert Hoovers, which were subjected to an onslaught such as their namesakes had never had to endure. Her ample frame made short work of the roses, and the thorns, for their part, had an ample target (Jessie was reputed to be 63-55-66 and 17 stone when in the natural).

Her howls brought Totty running. As Jessie lay writhing in agony, he chased the big bull all over her garden before managing to get hold of it. Making sure it was unhurt, he took it back to his pond and placed it gently amongst the reeds. He then returned to see what Jessie was making all the fuss about.

And so it went on. The local garbage wagon, loaded full and emitting not too attractive an odour, got stuck in the main street, right in front of the district sanitary inspector's house, because an outsize puddock had crawled up the exhaust pipe and got lodged.

Old Joe Twaddle picked up his watering can to give his greenhouse plants a drink and found he was "watering" them with frog spawn. Puddocks

Tales of Fishing and Fishermen

invaded kitchens, gummed up water taps and slept in milk bottles and sodden footwear - their spawn was to be found in every conceivable spot from one end of Troochie to the other.

Josie Thunk nearly had a thrombosis trying to separate the pages of the *Troochie Herald* and doors refused to open and tea-pot and kettle spouts were sealed with 100 per cent efficiency. Troochie had its first emergency in history. All-out war was declared on the invaders and Totty was ordered into the front line.

The war continued unabated but not enough headway was being made, and eventually three experts were called in to clear the neighbourhood of the invaders once and for all. Totty's pond was quickly filled in, the reeds dug out and the 600-odd frogs captured that day were transported to the pond up in the bog - whence their parents and some of them had come.

A wan smile crossed Totty's countenance when he heard this crumb of comfort, but he showed no trace of a smile when, one morning a few weeks later, he received a bill from the Council for £92 - " for clearing the village of a plague of frogs, for the presence of which, you, Totty McShin, were responsible."

The Rendezvous

"ROOSY" REID and BIG WULL LAMB, gentlemen of the road both, two of that ever-diminishing band which roams Scotland's highways and byways from Durness to the Mull of Galloway, bumped into each other one drizzly September morning on the A74. It was their first meeting for many months.

"Weel, noo, Wull," began Roosy. "Whaur the hell huve ye been a' this time? A thocht ye must huve emigrated tae England!"

"Nae bloody fears. A aye turn aboot whenever A get near tae Gretna Green. It's Scotland fur me every time. A dinnae unerstaun' the lingo efter Gretna an' they unerstaun' me even less."

"An' whaur are ye gaun noo?" asked Roosy.

"Weel, noo, A wiz kinda' intendin' tae daunder doon tae Lockerbie, an' then back up tae Glesca fur a bit. It's warmer in the big toons when the nichts are gettin' caulder."

"Aye, that's true, Wull. A micht jist gaun there masel!"

"Whit aboot gaun thegither then? We've never din that before."

"Ye're oan!" answered Roosy, "bit no' till the morn. A promised the farmer's wife whaur A'm stayin' near Abington that A wid saw some logs fur her later oan the day."

"Whit dae ye mean whaur ye're stayin'? Ye dinnae mean tae tell me ye've taken up permanent residence?"

"Oh no, nane o' that. Bit it's been kinda wet this last day or twa an' she's let me sleep in an auld henhoose her man had pit doon near the water. A've aye managed tae get a guid troot fur ma breakfast by settin' a line wi' a docken maggot at nicht, an' a bit rabbit fur ma denner noo an' again. Bit A feel the itch tae get movin' again, so Glesca let it be. The morn's mornin'?"

"Aye, fine man. Tell ye whut, Roosy, lad, A'm in an auld railway hut doon there at Beattock. A'll race ye tae Glesca. Jist fur a bit o' fun. We could meet at the Zoo yonder jist as ye gaun in. Bit nae gettin' lifts in big, fancy limousines, mind - jist cairts an' tractors."

Wull, not surprisingly, had never been lifted by a car in his life, but was an eternal optimist. Or a humorist.

"Richt!" answered Roosy. Considering the ramshackle appearance of the two men, with their massive unruly beards, odd boots and what looked like Crimean War greatcoats, Roosy had no need to make the obvious observation.

"An' whit aboot a wee wager?" suggested Wull, "Your new belt against ma guid hat?"

"Aye, a' richt. See ye at the Zoo. Bit dinnae gaun inside, mind, or A'll hae a job recognisin' ye amangst a' thae hairy..."

"A' richt, a' richt! An' come tae think o' it ye kinda look like yin yersel'!"

105

Tales of Fishing and Fishermen

Roosy tramped the few miles to the farm, sawed his logs, got something in the way of supper for his pains and bedded down early on a bunch of dry straw. Some of the hens followed him, perhaps wondering why someone was occupying their former abode, and two of them managed to get in before he closed the door for the night. He let them be, knowing they might be the source of a warm and nourishing breakfast. He wanted to be off at first light and it would delay his departure if he had to gut and cook a trout poached from the river.

Roosy soon lapsed into one of those deep, untroubled sleeps with which outdoor dwellers are often eternally blessed; and did not waken once during the course of the night. But this was surprising even so, because soon after eleven o'clock the drizzle, deciding that gentleness can be taken too far, became an unremitting downpour which pounded the bare hillsides and the tin roof of the henhouse hour after hour. The river, which was already running high, rose very fast and kept on rising, but Roosy slept on in his riverside retreat, unaware of what was happening.

Sometime around six o'clock he opened his eyes and felt the hut lurch and tilt. Puzzled because he could hear no wind, he got to his feet and looked out of the paneless window - and gulped. He was sailin' doon the Clyde, borne along in his ancient and fragile craft by a maelstrom which was apparently hellbent on pouring itself - and him - into the distant Atlantic.

At first alarmed, he decided, after the henhouse had successfully negotiated two or three pools and even intermittent rapids, that things could have been worse. Both hens had obliged, so he swallowed the eggs while they were still warm. He swallowed them as he stood gazing through the window that had become a porthole, and he felt like a captain on his bridge, scanning the waters that lay ahead.

With something in his stomach, he began to take an even more optimistic view of the situation.

He had always aspired to a trip on a boat and here he was, having a free sail and a sort of mystery cruise at that, although he did know vaguely where the Clyde ended up. He thought of Big Wull, plodding up the wet road, getting the occasional short lift on a car or bogey - if he was lucky.

Soon, as he was swept close to the bank and under a roadbridge, he glimpsed a signpost marked : BIGGAR 4.

And so it went on: CARSTAIRS 3...LANARK 2...CARLUKE 3....this was how to travel, to utilise the waterways as well as the roads. His fellow passengers just stood and swayed about, wondering what on earth was going on, giving the occasional cluck and eyeing him quizzically.

Each time the hut was driven into a sort of whirlpool, Roosy got slightly giddy and wet feet as well, as there was a fair gap between the bottom of the door and the floor, but he regained his composure when the various currents worked the hut back into the mainstream. One of the hens, understandably in the circumstances, laid again and Roosy poured back his third egg.

At one point the henhouse was forced to the very edge of a grass-fringed pool and Roosy could easily have opened the door and stepped ashore. But why should he? He was enjoying this unexpected cruise "doon the water". It was one of the highlights of his long years of vagabondage. And the glittering prize at the finishing post was that topper of a hat from Big Wull. His own had as many holes as a colander and would have been more useful as such than for the purpose for which it was originally designed. Not that Roosy ever strained anything, apart from his legs.

Gradually, the Clyde widened and slowed in tempo. Anglers, attracted out by the floodwater and the prospects of an easy kill on the worm, had appeared on its banks, all taking their eyes off their rods to marvel at the sight of the errant henhouse. Roosy, not sure of what would happen if he let it be known it had a crew, a one-man one, kept away from the window whenever there was the possibility of his being observed.

As the nautical miles were clocked up, the scenery had changed from stark hills to undulating fields, then to villages and towns and factories, to even bigger factories and large tenements and high-rise flats. Roosy was coming in to port.

Eventually, he drifted down past that well-known and once so important Glasgow offshoot, with its panorama of giant cranes calling to mind, though not to his, the splendid days of the great passenger ships that, sadly, have long since gone and no doubt for ever.

The wash from what must have looked to him like a huge ocean liner, but was in fact a small tug, sent his own craft careering shorewards. Roosy jumped on to dry land with a bemused hen under each arm. The henhouse, caught in the back lash, moved out into midstream and was now destined for the Atlantic and a fate unknown.

Roosy stopped to ponder. The downstream journey from Abington had taken a mere nine hours. Big Wull would be fortunate to have reached Douglas Moor. He had plenty of time, perhaps days. Even so, better to get to the Zoo and arrange for a gateman to testify to the hour and day of his arrival. Then he could explore the immediate area.

But he was wrong. For one thing, he had overshot his destination and had to footslog it southwards to get to the agreed rendezvous. And he knew nothing of the benign way in which Dame Fortune had also smiled upon his friend.

As it happened, the deluge of the previous night had come pouring through the roof of Big Wull's railside lodgings to give him both a rude awakening and a premature or, more accurately, unaccustomed face-wash. So he got up and crawled under a tarpaulin in a goods wagon lying in a siding at Beattock where, in spite of his discomfort, he succumbed once more to deep sleep. When he re-awoke around dawn, it was to the sound of clanking wheels as his conveyance, along with some twenty others, was hauled away towards the great city to the north. He looked out, chuckled and stayed where he was.

Tittering with delight, he hopped off when the train, after numerous halts and a pathetic average speed, came to a final grinding stop in the centre of Glasgow toon. He, too, had overshot his mark but he found his bearings and made for the Zoo.

The two tramps converged simultaneously on their pre-arranged destination, each incredulous on seeing the other. But a tie was declared. Roosy kept his belt and Big Wull his hat. And each of them his self-esteem, such as it was.

As Roosy proudly showed Big Wull his two hens, his companion reciprocated by revealing that his ample hessian sack was half-filled with best-grade BR coal. They found a derelict house with a view of the Clyde through the girders and enjoyed lashings of roast chicken and a blazing fire. And, after such a regal feast in such comfortable surroundings, they felt it a matter of course that they should indulge in an after-dinner discussion, during which they puffed contentedly at cigarettes made from newspaper and other people's discarded ends and exchanged views on the relative merits of travel by boat and rail.

Not far off, in a sumptuous city hotel, some of the guests were complaining at that very moment about the chill in the centrally-heated dining room, the drabness of the six-course menu and the fact that there was no fresh salmon. Couples argued heatedly and pouted and sulked over domestic problems concerning new cookers and freezers and dish-washers, or where in the tropics they should spend their autumn break.

The Swindlers

THE ROUGH, rocky estuary of the turbulent little Tannich had always been famous for its seals, so much so that the creatures constituted a tourist attraction. Then gradually they began to disappear. Everyone wondered why. Everyone except Tuggy Madden and Sammy Nimmo.

Tug and Sam started off in their enterprising business venture in a small way, but success, as they say, breeds, and it was not long before they were spending a lot of their time in February and March hauling out kelts from the deep holding pools with bunches of worms and then hawking "choice salmon steaks" round the big housing estates in Glasgow and Edinburgh and Dundee and even south of the Border, the latter market made easily accessible with the completion of the A74 and the M6.

It was wonderful how a touch of red colouring could improve the pale, jaundiced flesh of a thoroughly debauched kelt, and it was very seldom that housewives had the opportunity to get hold of "fresh spring salmon" at 90 pence a pound. In any case, most of the partnership's clientèle had never partaken of such a dainty dish, only heard of it. City people knew nothing about kelts, being even ignorant of the word.

Tuggy and Sammy soon found they were on to a good thing and expanded their "business" to take about 150 lb. of "salmon" on each safari into the jungle of the great housing schemes. As true sons of the shadier side of the Welfare State, they were both drawing unemployment benefit and, in addition, could show a net profit of about £80 every two days. They had had to purchase a van, and in the less lucrative days, when the enterprise was in its infancy, they had often obtained their petrol by syphoning it from other people's tanks.

Nor did they always return empty. Often they managed to pick something up - literally - on the way back: coils of wire, planks of wood, concrete slabs, coping stones, barrows, tools - they usually got their hands on something, simply hating the idea of running an empty vehicle. Like so many of their fellow beings, they had that common human failing of never being satisfied. Good profits, even illegally gained, were not enough. Their philosophy was that of continual grasp and grab, even till their fingers ached.

Some of the purchasers of the fish found the flavour a little different from what they had expected, but not belonging to the gourmet breed, and hence unaccustomed to gastronomic delicacies, they were in no position to argue, their subtle summing-up of the meal being that it fell far short of mince and tatties, or tripe and trotters, according to the area in which the partnership was operating. However, the occasional connoisseur knew he (or she) had been swindled and it was the potential threat from this type that made Tug and Sam decide never to visit the same housing complex twice. And so vast

Tales of Fishing and Fishermen

and numerous were the council estates stretching from Central Scotland to Lancashire and Yorkshire that they had no difficulty in keeping to this golden rule.

One day in late February, having already "done" parts of Dundee and Edinburgh earlier that week, they sped along the new highway bound for the sprawling new suburban areas of Glasgow. They were tempted to stop and try their luck in a town lying half-way between home and their destination, but on seeing an angler with a spinning-rod, they thought better of it and pushed on citywards.

They were expecting a bumper profit from their bumper load of almost 200 lb. of steaks, duly prepared with the pink colouring, since the previous day the water had been very low and the kelts had been lying so thick in the narrow rock pools that they hadn't even had to use worms. Bare trebles had sufficed.

Business was brisk in the monolithic scheme on the eastern outskirts of Scotland's greatest city - until a large and irate housewife (whose son worked in the kitchen of a large Clydeside hotel and sneaked home a cut of fresh salmon now and again) came storming back to the van soon after making her purchase, her great bosom heaving menacingly and her beetroot-red face registering her willingness to launch forth into the direst of battles if the occasion demanded.

"Ca' this salmon! It's a lump o' dirty cod. An' as dry as a stick! An' it's had the measles - or somethin' worse." (At this juncture Big Bella pointed to one or two red smears on the flesh). "Gie's ma money back - double, or A'll git the polis."

In their hurry to prepare their larger than usual consignment, Tug and Sam had obviously omitted to give at least one of the steaks the full treatment. Wishing to quell this female tornado who, with her raucous voice and belligerent posture could obviously bring them no end of trouble, Tuggy pressed a £1 note into her dirty big palm.

"Sorry, mad'dum, A must have made a mistake some place ...."

"Aye, when ye went tae some rubbish dump instead o' the fish market."

"Mad-dum" took the £1 and Tuggy, by way of interest, took the "choice salmon" steak across his right eye:-

"There's a poultice fur ye. Ye'll mebbe see better whit ye're sellin' efter this."

Tuggy staggered back against one of the trays, which was dislodged and its contents pitched into a large-size puddle on the road. The water immediately turned a bright red.

"Jist look at that!" roared Big Bella, now joined by two of her cronies from the same stair who had also purchased 90 pence steaks as a special treat to accompany their evening's quota of stout. "That fish hiz been pentit! Whaur's the polis?"

"Sssh, mad'dum, sssh!" Tug and Sam implored the ladies on bended knees and sodden lumps of kelt not to "git the polis." But Big Bell and Mad Meg and fiery Wee Teenie were just as astute at taking advantage of a promising situation as their adversaries. Bella applied the screw:-

"Ten quid each, then."

"Whit?"

"Ye heard, ten quid. An' think yersels lucky at that. Ye'd better hurry up, tae. See whit A see comin'?"

True enough, the giant unmistakable figure of a member of the Glasgow Constabulary was walking towards them, eyeing the scene.

The partnership needed no more prodding. Six £5 notes were hastily pulled from inner pockets and handed over. And as Bella and her lieutenants made a bee-line for the off-licence, the steaks were scooped from the puddle and thrown into the van which was crunched into gear and set in motion.

Just in case a police car had been sent after them, Tuggy and Sammy stopped at the first suitable ditch and ejected what was now a highly dangerous cargo, ready to explode in their faces. The local rats had a whale of a feast that night.

For the first time ever they had made a loss on the two-days' work - and a substantial one at that. They did not like it.

When similar and equally disconcerting incidents occurred in Bolton and Manchester and were mentioned on TV news and in the national press, the firm of Madden and Nimmo went into involuntary liquidation, wisely deciding to call it a day, at least as far as sales to human consumers were concerned. For a spring or two their loads of kelts went to one or two pig-farmers but they eventually came to the conclusion that the low rate the latter paid did not justify the risk involved. They went into the scrap-iron business, ironically scraping away the red rust to increase the market value of their wares, whereas before they had applied a similar colour for the very same purpose.

And the seals gradually returned to the estuary.

The Fly Man

GEOFFREY RICKINGHAM presented the perfect picture of the accomplished angler - at least in his own reckoning. Decked out in a loudly-checked sports jacket, with expensive Polaroids showing either from his breast pocket or hanging in ostentatious fashion from a silver chain, and wearing a Donegal bristling with almost every type of exotic trout fly imaginable, most of them quite unimaginable (the latter fashioned by his own hand), he would strut, like the most pompous of peacocks, round every southern reservoir he visited, telling everyone what flies they should be using, where they should be casting, how they should be varying their approach according to the height of the sun. the strength of the wind or the density of the cloud. In short, he was one of those "anglers" who seem to derive their greatest pleasure, not from actual fishing, but from dictating to their fellows and trying to impress them with tales of magnificent catches gained through the application of original tactics in combination with brilliant fly design. And, of course, it was not by sheer coincidence that he sold large numbers of his gaudy inventions to the ignorant, the uninitiated and the impressionable who, at a moment when reservoir fishing in particular was attracting more and more raw recruits, were hungry for knowledge and success and prepared to pay lip-service to any raving lunatic who chanced to come along.

So when the ubiquitous Rickingham moved out of home territory into the northern neighbourhood of Achnadoig, where hard-bitten fishers almost outnumbered the trout population of the local loch and the news of the capture of a heavy fish on fly was at once passed orally from door to door, he found the angling populace cocked a much less willing ear than the hordes of well-meaning but unknowledgeable débutants who had been in the majority at the man-made reservoirs whence he had come.

Some treated him with the rudeness which he at least in part deserved. On advising Fergus McAlistair, during one of his waterside inspections of others' equipment (when, as usual, the degree of pontification had to be heard to be believed), that his flies were too small and of too dull a colour, he was reminded by the down-to-earth Fergie that flies attached to a cast and worked over the surface of a loch were much more likely to attract a fish than those impaled in a Donegal hat, irrespective of their size or their pattern. Others were less polite, less tolerant, telling him to go and stick his Rickingham's Rocket, his Rickingham's Revel and his Rickingham's Rat-a-Tat in a place where, had he complied, they certainly would have constituted no threat to any trout anywhere. Rickingham may have done well selling his multi-coloured improbabilities to the gullible beginners of the English reservoirs, but the habitués of Loch Achnadoig were of a different breed.

They knew exactly which species of fly was likely to be blown from the hillsides on to the loch at any given time of year, and most of them had seen the heather bloom and fade too often even to chew over, far less swallow, the extravagant outpourings of an incomer who, they were genuinely beginning to think, must be an escapee from an institution for mentally disarranged anglers. Certainly they had seen nothing that remotely resembled any of the bizarre creations he claimed to be fish-catching "flies", except perhaps when, after an evening spent down at the Black Antlers, they had partaken much too generously of their favourite Island Mist or Stalkers' Joy and were strolling home, pleasantly confused and apt to see familiar creatures wildly distorted by their intake of pure Highland gold. But, as old Rury McNab observed in one of his more sober moments (which meant the remark was passed some time before midday): "Oor troots wid laugh their fins off if they saw thae things."

Yet, at the same time, they had to agree with Rickingham that their impoverished loch would benefit from heavy stocking. But how, with their limited financial resources?

The eccentric from the South came to the rescue. He explained that he had a cousin in Buckinghamshire, a big fish-farmer, who would supply him with rainbows at an almost give-away price. The actual figure was quoted and canny secretary Gussie McNaught, having laboriously inquired what the cost would be from other farms, reported to his committee that the offer was one that should not be missed. Many of the Highland hearts present fluttered at the thought of paying out money "fur thae tame, flabby rainbow troots" but at the same time, none of them, true to temperament, could happily turn themselves away from what appeared to be a highly favourable transaction. After all, Gussie argued, the hard conditions on windswept Loch Achnadoig would soon toughen the rainbows up and turn them into real trout, more like their native brothers. "Aye, if it disnae kill them a' off the first week," commented old Rury in a voice richly alcoholic.

But the pro-rainbow brigade won the day and a tin containing a large number of £1 notes was duly entrusted to "Daft Ricky," as he was now commonly known. But he was trailed all the way to the Post Office and observed at the counter from a distance of about 2 ft., just to make sure. After all, these men of Achnadoig were little accustomed to business deals, and since leaving the village school the only time Gussie put pen (or, rather, pencil) to paper was on a memorable occasion each year when he nailed a painfully scrawled notice of the annual general meeting - not that he called it that - to the door of the hut at the head of the loch. Needless to say, the keeping of minutes would have been an intellectual exercise too demanding even to be considered, and no record of meetings existed. If any dates or figures had to be borne in mind, they were usually scratched on an inside wall of the hut. And, in any case, members' memories were long - and accurate.

The trout were of about 1 lb. each, and the worthies of Achnadoig watched excitedly and rubbed their hands together in gleeful anticipation as the fish were carefully deposited in their beloved loch.

The following evening the club was out in force. Although some had felt the new stock should be given a week or two to settle, not one had the slightest idea of the way in which these fish had been reared back in the stewponds of Buckinghamshire, and Maestro Rickingham did nothing to enlighten them ...

Fifty pence was collected by Gussie from each member, again on the suggestion of the instigator of the scheme, who explained that such an event was always celebrated with a competition, the total sum staked being the prize for the heaviest catch. It wasn't often that such a feverish pitch of excitement hit the sleepy village of Achnadoig ...

Soon the Gussies and the Rurys, the Sandys and the Robbies were led to wonder whether Daft Ricky might not have been right with his crazy theories and wild concoctions after all. While they toiled and sweated without reward, casting their March Browns and Black Spiders and Blue Duns in the area where the fish had been placed, Geoffrey Rickingham stood some distance away, obviously unable to put a fly wrong. He was slaughtering them.

"Thae troots must be as bloody daft as him if they tak' thae things he ca's flees!" said Gussie in a voice seething with disgust. "An' look hoo he's fishin'!" He's whippin' the flees back oot just efter they hit the water!"

Many of the Achnadoigans, now convinced they had made a colossal blunder in condemning the newcomer as a blithering idiot as far as fishing was concerned, moved in a solid mass towards the spot where he was gradually filling his creel and, as they did so, Rickingham moved away, keeping his distance. Some sneaked in ahead of him, hardly maintaining the agreed 25 ft. between rods. But it made no difference. At the end of the evening, while Rickingham's basket was bursting with rainbows, theirs held only air and unfulfilled hopes.

Ricky collected his first prize, which went a long way towards compensating him for all the abuse he had suffered from those he had tried to instruct. But he also collected a pretty penny from the sales of his flamboyant Rockets and Revels and Rat-a-Tats, sheepishly requested by those who until now had been his mocking detractors.

Then, a few days later, he quietly disappeared from the scene.

But those who fished the loch with his fancy fabrications met with scant success and gradually resorted to their old orthodox patterns, with which they now regularly killed trout, some of which rapidly reached the 2 lb. mark. Isolated as they were from the latest trends in the angling world, they were not to know that hand-reared rainbows take time to adjust to the natural food supplies of a new environment, and that while being reared in stewponds, they are regularly fed with growth-inducing pellets.

Nor were they to know that each time Rickingham had unhooked a fish from one of his "daft-lookin' flees" on that first evening, he had furtively pressed a couple of spherical offerings on to the point of the iron.

Wet Wit?

FOR A SCORE of years Wee Eck and Big Cherlie had enjoyed, or suffered, depending on the circumstances, one of those love-hate relationships which are perhaps more common amongst members of the fishing fraternity than is generally believed. For weeks on end, their devotion to each other, even in the most trivial matters, would be boundless. Then, for some unaccountable reason, the disagreements and the niggling would start. And an explosion was often the outcome.

After hours of teeming rain early one July, the Poochie promised to be in rollicking flood the next day, which prompted the suggestion from Cherlie that they get out the old tandem and cycle the twelve miles to the upper reaches, where the brown trout, unharried by those who were not inclined to make such a strenuous journey and were content to spend their time on the tortured waters near the village, were fat and golden and fairly plentiful. But Wee Eck had, for an angler, an unusual hatred of wet weather, and his enthusiasm for the proposed outing wasn't exactly boundless.

"Ach, A'm no' gaun fishin' the morn, Cherlie. There's gaun tae be mair rain an' ye ken hoo A hate fishin' in the wet. Yer haunds git a' claurty wi' worms an' yer piece looks like somethin' oot o' somebody's rubbish pail an' yer fag's like a piece o' breid that's been steeped a' nicht in the sink. A'm no' like you, A'm particular, ye ken. A dinnae care much fur worm juice an' worm skins oan ma piece, especially if the worms came oot o' Auld Lizzie's midden. An' A'll tell ye somethin' else - A aye feel queer fur a day or twa efter A've goat wet tae the skin. A git kinda nightmares in the middle o' the nicht."

Big Cherlie, who always seemed to be quite impervious to any form of physical discomfort and who had been known, when he forgot his billy can, to empty the contents of his worm tin into some other convenient receptacle and then to use it to brew his tea (although in all fairness it must be admitted that he usually gave it a cursory swirl in the burn), looked disdainfully at his friend:

"Ach, Eck man, ye're only a fair weather fisher. A wee bit o' rain wull never harm ye. Are ye frichtit ye'll melt an' disappear intae the grund? An' hoo the hell can gettin' wet gie ye nightmares? It's mair likely tae be a' that raw whisky ye git frae that chap at the distillery. Oanyway, there'll no' be much mair rain efter a' the heavy stuff we've had. A'll bring the bike o'er at the back o' echt o'clock in the mornin'. A' richt?"

"Well, mebbe this time A'll risk it. Bit if it comes oan rain A'll want tae gaun hame an' wi' us huving the tandem, that means ye'll huve tae come hame tae. A' richt?"

"Well a' richt, a' richt. We'll see." (The last sentence was uttered in an inaudible whisper).

Wet Wit?

But Wee Eck's gloomy forethought about the following day's weather was proved to be correct. Soon after they'd covered the long, uphill road to their favourite stretch of the Poochie and with only a solitary fish in each basket, the skies opened to unleash upon them what was little less than an unremitting deluge.

Wee Eck took about 30 seconds to express his feelings:

"Aw," he moaned, "A'm awa' hame. The water's rinnin' doon ma neck an' oot o' ma sleeves an' bits. The last time A wiz oot in stuff like this there wiz a bloody eel in ma hip pocket when A got hame an' A couldnae even smoke ma pipe tae comfort me when A wiz dried oot for the bloody thing had eten a' ma baccy. Nae winder A wiz huvin' awfu' dreams aboot big congers swallowin' me up in yin big gulp an' then spittin' me oot in wee bits. S'nae..."

"A'm no' surprised they spat ye oot!" interrupted Big Cherlie.

"Less o' yer cheek! A wiz gaun tae say it's nae use oanyway, water's too claurty an' it's sae wet we'd be as weel stanin' oot in the burn up tae oor necks. A want tae gaun hame, so c'moan. We'll git oot o' here an' oan the bloody auld bike."

"Bit ach, Eck man, it'll mebbe gaun off."

"Gaun off? Aye, efter we've been droont. C'moan!"

"Ach, Eck, A think thae troots'll come oan yet. A wid like tae bide a while longer."

"Bit that wiznae oor arrangement, wiz it? Ye promised that if it got wet ye wid gaun hame if A wanted tae."

"Aye, bit when A said that A didnae ken it wiz gaun tae rain, did A? A'll tell ye whit - you tak' the tandem hame noo an' git Geordie tae bring it up the nicht fur me tae come hame. A' richt?" (Geordie was Wee Eck's 30-year-old son).

"A suppose so".

"Bit nae later than echt o'clock, mind. A'm no' meanin' tae stay here a' nicht, ye ken."

"Ye'll be sproutin' bloody fins if ye dae. Ye'll no' need a bike - ye'll be able tae swim back doon hame."

So Eck departed with his single fish for drier surroundings, while Cherlie went on meting out a lingering death to his blackheaded worms, hoping the downpour would put the water up again and bring the fish properly on to the feed.

But it did neither. The pounding rain was extremely localised, and in fact the trout became dourer than ever. Cherlie began to get thoroughly fed up and, by mid-afternoon, eight o'clock seemed to be a half-a-century away. By the time the appointed hour did come round, he felt as if even his bones had gone to mush and he looked like something the river had brought down. His

Tales of Fishing and Fishermen

tea and "piece" had been finished around midday and the only addition to his catch was a puny 8-inch trout.

Quarter past eight came along, but no Geordie. Nine o'clock, and still no Geordie. By that time, Big Cherlie was just about at screaming pitch and had a murderous glint in his eye.

Unknown to him, Geordie, feeling a bit weak in the legs after propelling the tandem mostly uphill for over seven miles, and wetter than he had ever been in his life, had stopped at the lonely Grouse and Pheasant to buy some refreshment and hence to get some power back into his weary limbs. But there in the bar he had met a couple of former colleagues, farm-labourers like himself, and the whisky flowed so regularly and so copiously that well before eight o'clock Geordie had no idea how he chanced to be in the Grouse and Pheasant in the first place. By half-past eight he didn't even know he was in the Grouse and Pheasant. At nine o'clock he somehow managed to climb on to the tractor habitually used as transport by his rustic friends and after a ride during the course of which he was more than once nearly pitched into the roadway (although he was in far too advanced a state of inebriation even to realise it), he was deposited only a few hundred yards from the paternal roof. Some strange homing instinct ensured that he reached the front door.

Just after nine, Big Cherlie, on whom it had finally dawned that Geordie might not be coming, was foaming at the mouth. He squelched his way to the road, hoping he would be fortunate enough to thumb a lift back to the village, but the only motorists were strangers who could hardly have been censured for refusing to pick up such a bedraggled-looking apology for a human being.

Almost five hours later, towards two o'clock in the morning, he finally reached the shelter of his abode, dried himself off and collapsed into his bed. In his deep slumber, he strangled Wee Eck and Geordie at least half-a-dozen times.

When Wee Eck got up early in the morning, he went outside to check that the tandem was in the lean-to. Worried at not finding it where it should have been, and hearing raucous noises coming from Geordie's bedroom, he threw the door wide open and through the alcoholic haze could make out his son lying on his back, his mouth wide open and emitting the loudest snores he had ever heard.

"Hell, if he's here, whaur can the bloody tandem be?" he asked himself.

He shook his son into wakefulness:

"Whaur's the bloody bike?"

"Bike? Whit bike?" queried Geordie after the question had been put three times and he was at last conscious enough for it to register.

"The bloody tandem - whaur is it?"

"The tandem? Oh hell, A must huve left it at the pub. A got a lift frae Tam Stevenson oan the tractor."

"Bit ye were supposed tae gaun up tae the burn wi' the tandem tae bring Big Cherlie hame!"

"Oh hell, so A wiz. A mind noo."

"Ye stupit drunken lout! Whit dae ye think Big Cherlie's gaun tae say tae this? He'll huve oor guts fur worm casts."

"Ach hell. Big Cherlie! Oanybody can mak' a mistake. He shid huve came back wi' you."

"Aye, mebbe, bit he didnae an' you were supposed tae gaun fur 'um. He'll tear us intae wee bits. A think A'll rin awa' up intae the hills an' hide!"

"Aw, dinnae be sae daft, faither. There's twa o' us. If he comes roond here we can stand up tae 'um."

"Naw we cannae! He's the size o' baith o' us pit thegither an' a guid bit mair. He'll turn us ootside in! A'm awa' tae hae a guid dram oot o' that bottle A keep below the stair. A'll mebbe feel better fur it."

In the early afternoon, a series of thumping blows on the front door had Wee Eck quivering like a jelly while Geordie, in spite of his bold talk, turned ashen. Eck thought of diving under the bed, but he knew that this was an encounter that had to be faced sooner or later. Might as well get the pain over and done with.

Before he reached the door, it flew open under more hammer blows and Big Cherlie burst into the room. He grabbed father and son by their polo necks, one in each hand and, lifting them a foot off the floor, banged their heads together. Perhaps not surprisingly, the noise was like the crack of splitting timber and Eck and Geordie collapsed in a common heap, totally out for the count.

Big Cherlie picked up the two bodies and, in a manner which suggested they deserved no better treatment than sacks of rubbish, dumped them in the back of the pick-up he had borrowed for the occasion, then drove off along a narrow road and into the high hills. Twenty minutes later he turned on to a grassy track which he followed to a point where it lost itself in the steeply-rising ground. Then he unceremoniously pulled the now semi-conscious pair from the vehicle, deposited them in a small peat bog and departed to drive the twenty miles back to the village.

His mind was now at rest. He had reaped a full and satisfying revenge. Now they would know what it was like to be really soaked. Peat bogs didn't exactly make for a dry bed.

Five minutes after his departure, the pilot of a low-flying helicopter spotted two men waving frantically with one hand and holding their heads with the other. Injured climbers, he thought - and landed to pick them up.

Tales of Fishing and Fishermen

After only a few minutes they got out of the machine when it alighted on the space in front of their house.

Wee Eck was not slow to see that the situation was pregnant with possibilities. He could not resist such a temptation, and his innate sense of humour decreed that he would make the most of it.

He and Geordie had plenty of time to go and change their clothes and to be seated on Big Cherlie's doorstep when the latter arrived back with the pick-up - and he hadn't dawdled on the way.

When he saw the pair, he stopped dead in his tracks. You could have rammed a roadman's shovel into his mouth.

"Are we gaun tae the fishin' the morn, Cherlie?" asked Wee Eck in his normal voice.

"Hoo in hell's name! Naw, A cannae believe ma e'en! Hoo - hoo the hell? Naw, A'm seein' things. Aw Christ, hoo dae ye come tae be here?"

"Hoo dae we come tae be here? Hoo dae ye think? We jist walked roon frae the hoose tae apologise fur Geordie no' comin' fur ye last nicht. The chain broke in a thousand bits jist efter he left the hoose. He fell o'er the hanlebars an' got that big lump on his heid when he hit the kerb stane." (Eck's own outsize bump was concealed under a knitted toorie).

"Eh, whit? Whit are ye sayin'?"

"A'm sayin' A'm sorry aboot whit happened last nicht. Hoo did ye git hame?"

"Aw hell, A must be off ma heid!" groaned Cherlie.

"Whit d'ye mean?"

"A must huve goat hallucinations."

"Whit are them?"

"Ach, never mind." Cherlie was thinking that there could be only one possible explanation - that he had been affected by the thorough soaking in the same way as Wee Eck always was. Nightmares, hallucinations. Perhaps it was infectious.

It meant that there was no difference of opinion thereafter, Big Cherlie being even more convinced than Wee Eck that fishing in the wet was highly detrimental to both body and soul. Such a situation suited Eck down to the ground, and Cherlie still doesn't know the truth. And Wee Eck will try his damndest to ensure that he never will.

Yet Another Night to Remember

THE SEASONS had pursued each other as relentlessly as always - even faster than usual to those who had seen more than a few come and go - and once again it was October, and hence the month for the most memorable event in the Doonieburnie social calendar, the nerve-shattering, whisky-swilling, haggis-swallowing, skin-bruising mêlée that went under the somewhat pretentious name of the annual dinner dance of the local angling club. "Annual" was accurate enough. "Dinner"? The quality of the fare will reveal itself in due course. "Dance"? Well, it's a word which is open to a fairly wide interpretation.

Seamus Murdoch, secretary of the Doonieburnie Angling Club, the members of which constituted what was probably the wildest, and certainly the most colourful, group of fishers in the Highlands, had once again booked the village hall - the previous outing in a posh hotel had been a catastrophe - and hired the usual firm of so-called caterers to do the needful. The all-essential Booze presented no problem. The revellers brought massive supplies of their own usually palatable home-made malts like Darlin' Doonie and, this year, a new blend called Pauchle Puke. The Pauchle was the Doonie's main tributary and several hitherto unused additives had been introduced to produce this latest concoction, which connoisseurs of whisky would have said was aptly named.

"Whit's the grub the nicht?" bawled the insatiable Bogey Broon as soon as he had got one massive foot inside the hall. Bogey had but recently arrived from a neighbouring glen to take up residence in the village. "Nane o' that pigswill A get at hame, A hope, or that fancy Froggie rubbish A hear ye got last year."

It could be said in all seriousness that to the most fastidious gourmet the contents of a sow's trough, at least before the pig had mauled it up, would by no means have looked unattractive when compared to the revolting offal dished out to him each evening by the gormless and parsimonious sister with whom he lived. To poor Bogey, any meal, however pedestrian, however badly cooked, taken outside the confines of his cottage, was invariably a sumptuous banquet. But he was just a little apprehensive, because he had heard that the victuals offered at the annual social were sometimes just that little bit below *Cordon Bleu* standard.

The waiters, eying their guests with some trepidation, started to bring in the big ashets and the plates...

But wee Davy Craw, who never could relish the fodder offered until he had his taste buds whetted and his stomach well-lined with the nectar of the glens (or of one glen in particular), decided he had not yet imbibed enough antidote and reached down for his outsize bottle of Darlin' Doonie, held

tightly on the floor between his feet. In his haste, he leaned forward just at the moment when the redoubtable Slugger Thompson, that untamed and untameable giant whose facial features suggested that life had not been without its ups and downs, mainly downs, was eyeing, elbows on the table, his heaped first course in silent and enjoyable anticipation of the first gorgeous mouthful. But, unfortunately, Davy's arm caught his elbow and, before Slugger could take remedial action, he was brought into earlier contact with the contents of his plate than he had anticipated. His face went down into it at a speed that was unknown until someone broke the sound barrier, and when he had recovered sufficiently to carefully withdraw it, he was blinded, half-choked, and the possessor of a physiognomy which defied description, because to say it was a dripping, multi-coloured mess would have been something of an understatement.

Slowly, Slugger's fingers went to his eyes to scoop out what he could of the haggis, beetroot and turnips that were clouding his vision. Then, once he felt he could see well enough to take the first steps towards revenge, with compound interest, of course, he stared, as was his manner on such occasions, and without uttering a single word, at wee Davy. Then, unhurriedly and with his eyes fixed on what was his first target of the night, he rose menacingly to his feet. There was a general hush and forks and knives stopped half-way between plates and gaping mouths...

"Ye stupit wee galoot!" he roared in a voice which had the rafters groaning in protest and caused a flake or two of plaster to drop on top of the gathering. Catching Davy by the collar with his massive fist, he sent him reeling, right into the ample lap of Big Teenie McTavish, Doonieburnie's *enfant terrible*. As soon as Davy had touched down, Teenie grabbed him by his luxurious coiffure and accurately placed his distraught face slap in the middle of a large ashet full of liquid turnip. He extracted himself, looking for all the world like an anaemic jelly-fish.

Meanwhile the voracious Bogey Broon roared for a waiter:

"Mair haggis, hurry up!"

The waiter, unaccustomed to such boorish treatment, but wise enough to comply without comment, returned at once with a large plate covered in slices, six inches in diameter and half-an-inch thick, of Bogey's favourite dish. The latter grabbed a handful of them and rammed a whole one into the great gaping cavern that nature had allotted him between nose and chin.

It sounded - and to him it felt - as if he had closed his avid teeth on something that had come out of a foundry.

"Whit the hell's this?' he bellowed, a horse shoe?" And, withdrawing the apology for haggis with raking fingers and laying it flat against his open hand, he proceeded to flatten, block-buster fashion, the waiter's very

122

prominent nose, achieving in a fraction of a second what it would have taken a plastic surgeon a few hours to accomplish.

"Ca' that haggis, ye snottery wee loon? Whaur did ye get it? At the smiddy?"

Fiery wee Lizzie Glen, unjustifiably proud of the new dress she had made with her own hands and was wearing for the first time, was pointing out to her neighbour, Hannah Tosh, what to Lizzie were the delicate intricacies of its bodice, when swarthy Trabbie Tulloch, seated right opposite her, was in the act of taking a gigantic swig from his bottle of black rum (he was the sole Doonieburnian who preferred something else to whisky, a strange fact that was attributed by his fellows to suspected Jamaican blood in his veins) when a passing waiter, struggling under a heavy tray, staggered a foot to the left. The edge of the tray caught Trabbie in the nape of the neck and so great was the impetus that his whole head was pushed forward. At that very moment his beloved rum was running thick and sticky between his missing front teeth and the back of his throat, and, with explosive force, the entire intake, which must have amounted to a good quarter-pint, was ejected in a single jet, a foot long, to hit plumb in the centre, the most dangerous target that he could have chosen - the bodice of Lizzie's cherished home-made dress. The strong, pungent fluid soon altered radically both its colour and its texture.

For a brief moment Lizzie just could not believe her eyes. Then, realising in all its horror the full import of what had happened - the ruination of what to her had been expensive material, the hours of painstaking work, the spoiling of her evening's enjoyment - she began her act of awesome retaliation by ramming her pointed shoe with lightning force into Trabbie's left shin, a part of his anatomy which was exceptionally tender and caused him acute suffering when even the slightest draft blew up his trouser leg. This sorry state of affairs was due to the fact that the year before, in his piggery, he had collided in bone-grinding fashion with his ill-tempered boar, which he called King Kong. So Trabbie roared with the searing pain and collapsed in an inert heap, spreadeagled across the table.

But that was no more than a prelude on Lizzie's part. She was just getting steam up, just preparing her victim for the *coup de grâce*. Standing up to her full 4 ft. 10 in., she grabbed her handbag and, swinging it round bolas-fashion by the straps, she brought it down like a ton of bricks - which, by the weight of it, might well have been its contents - on top of the smoothest and baldest pate that Doonieburnie had ever known. And to the agony of his throbbing shin and the agony of his bruised cranium was added the agony of a somewhat disjointed nose because as his head went down tablewards, it was on a certain collision course with the huge pepper-pot with which he had been about to endeavour to put some taste into his neeps. Its pointed top

Tales of Fishing and Fishermen

forced its way half-way up one nostril, knocking completely out of perspective what had not been a very becoming nose in the first place.

Trabbie, suffering from multiple wounds and with vivid recollections of El Alamein, crawled away from the fray and huddled, shell-shocked, in a corner. There he could lick his sores in peace.

At the end of the meal, by which time all the members of the company, even those who were showing obvious scars of battle, had attained their accustomed pinnacle of joviality, Seamus, confident that the evening was once again a howling success, rose unsteadily to his feet:

"Geentilmen and ladies, here we are a' here noo once again, wi' oor bellies pushin' oot oor belts after that grand feed...."

This exquisitely original beginning to his speech, expressed as it was in truly magnificent rhetoric, was rudely interrupted. Some people simply do not appreciate the subtle beauties of the English language:

"A whit? They forgot tae wring oot the neeps an' A've pit ma haggis in ma pocket for tae patch ma moleskins wi' when A git hame. An' whaur did they get the coostard? Oot o' thae craws' nests doon at the Auld Brig? The tinkers up at the loch widnae gie that stuff tae thur mongerel dugs. An' thur dugs are no' a' that choosy. A can tell ye, A've seen yin o' them wolfin' doon a hedgehug."

He who uttered such harsh criticism was Danny Stock, who professed to be an authority on things gastronomical and at the same time a connoisseur of the finest liqueurs. In actual fact, his staple diet was stovies and mince and the roughest brew of Pauchle Puke that the village had yet produced. It was known to have temporarily floored a young bull on which he had tried it out. He knew if the bull didn't succumb, his own chances of survival were pretty good.

"Noo, please, geentilmen, nae interructions, please, p-l-e-a-s-e!" pleaded Seamus. "We want tae get oan wi' the persentation o' the prizes for last season."

"It'll be a fix as usual," interrupted Slugger Thompson.

"Nae interructions I said, p-l-e-a-s-e. First prize for the heaviest salmon gauns tae that immacoolate angler, Josie Flunk, for the beautiful 22-punder he took oot o' the Chanty oan a hame-made flee."

"Beaut-i-ful?" bawled Henny McNab. "A saw it! A thocht it wiz a pike that had been through a' the tubs in the dye-hoose."

"An' oan a home-made flee?" queried Shugh Tarff. "It wiz made at the smiddy by Cast-Iron Cherlie an' if that wiz a flee A'm a 20-antlered stag. It wiz a four-inch long copper door hinge wi' six great trebles oan it, an' you could see by the fish whaur he had hooked it - by the belly. Half its puddins wiz hangin' oot when he tug-o'-war'd it oan tae the bank."

"Noo, noo, nane o' that," implored Seamus. "Josie got the fish fair an' square."

"Aye, fair an' square in the guts," persisted Shugh.

"P-l-e-a-s-e stop interructin', Shugh. Noo folks, if Josie will step forward A have a very special prize for him. A had a lot o' bother organisin' it but A am sure Josie will appreciate this great new idea in oor prizes, an idea which me as your secretary thocht up oot o' ma ain heid."

This item of news was greeted with a wondering silence. They could expect anything now if it came "oot o' Seamus' heid".

Josie, puzzled and not a little perturbed by the words he had just heard, ambled forward to the top table where Seamus stood beaming as he approached. The secretary lifted an envelope which lay before him and a questioning hush again fell on the assembly. An envelope? Usually the prize was a parcel containing waders, or a rod or a net. Could it be one of those cheque things? What could Josie do with that? Any bank seeing him approach would bar up its doors immediately and call the Riot Squad.

Gingerly, as if it might have been a letter-bomb, Josie took the envelope, examined it and prised it open. He read it aloud - he read everything aloud, following each syllable with his finger - and everyone hung on every word:

"Permission for one rod to fish the No. 5 Beat of the Sh- She- Sheen for the two days February twentieth and twenty-first...."

Josie stared unbelievingly at Seamus, then gulped:

"Whit's this, a joke? Whit is it? Whaur the hell's the Sheen?"

"Och, Josie, man, the **Shin** is in Sutherland, aboot a hunder miles."

"A hunder miles? A'm no bikin' a hunder miles for oany fishin'. The last time A went a long road oan ma bike there wiz a gale blawin' in ma face. There A wiz prayin' fur it tae change richt roon fur me oan the way back an' unlucky fur me it didnae." This quite irrational and somewhat puzzling statement was met with loud guffaws from those who were not yet too intoxicated - or too bereft of grey matter - to see its comic implications. Josie halted momentarily, wondering what had caused the laughter, then he proceeded:

"Look, A'm no' wantin' oany fishin' oan oany stupit Sheen or whutever ye ca' it. The Doonie an' the Pauchle'll dae me. Ye can stick yer Sheen...."

"Noo, noo, Josie son, nane o' that stuff. Nae blaspheemy in here. There A thocht A wiz daein' ye a great favour by gaun tae a' this bother - A even had tae write a letter. You loons dinnae appreciate oanything that's din for ye. A'm fed up aye bein' criticised for daein' the wrong thing. A ken we've a' got oor burdens tae bear but A sometimes wonder whut A've din tae deserve you lot."

"Aw rubbish!" Josie, having squashed the permit in his grubby fist,

Tales of Fishing and Fishermen

grabbed Seamus with the other hand and rammed the offending piece of paper down the secretary's polo neck, adding:

"Ye can gaun tae the Sheen yersel'. An' if ye dinnae come back A'll no' be worried. But afore ye gaun ye can get me a new pair o' waders for ma prize. That's whit A need. Wi' the yins A've got noo when A walk intae the water it soons like the wa' ootside Jenny McGritty's bar at closin' time oan a Saturday nicht an'..."

"Noo, noo, Josie, nane o' that stuff."

"A' richt, if ye promise me a new pair o' waders!"

"Aw, shut yer goblet!" squawked Caw-Caw-Candless. "Ye poached the fish oanyway."

"A did nut! It took ma horseshoe."

"So that's whit ye ca' it. It certainly looked a bit like yin. Whit did ye use for a rod - a windlass?"

"Sssh, folks, sssh!" beseeched Seamus. "A'll have a word wi' oor freend Josie later oan. Noo, let's get oan tae the winner o' the prize for the biggest troot."

"An' whit ye gi'en him?" roared Josie. "A ticket for some burn oan the moon?"

"Silence, please, an' nae sarcatasm. The winner o' the prize for the biggest broon troot gauns once again tae that grand handler o' a greenhert an' the greatest drooner o' worms Doonieburnie has ever seen - the one and only Mister McCann. His troot o' fower an' a hauf punds wiz caught in the month o' May oan a wee water wi' a wee brumle worm. Canny wiz usin' three-punds breakin' strain an' a No. 18 hook an' it took him twinty meenits tae get the fish oot. A great achievement."

"Three-punds breakin' strain? A size 18 hook? Is that whut he telt ye? Listen, Seamus, A wiz there that mornin'. He saw that fish lyin' between twa rocks. He thocht it wiz a grilse an' he drew a shark hook intae it, tied tae a claethes rope. He should get done for poachin' an' there ye are gi'en him a prize."

"That's richt!" roared Lochie Laidlaw. "Ma troot o' twa an a hauf punds should get the prize. A caught it fair an' square."

"Blethers!" Yet another mock irate voice chimed in. "He stole it oot o' a shop in Inverness. Ma wife's sister's niece's man saw him. He slipped it doon inside his troosers. Can ye no' smell them?"

It was the usual fiasco - argument, counter-argument, jovial and not-so-jovial banter. But Seamus was used to the uninhibited conduct of his rebellious protégés and always managed to restore at least a temporary semblance of law and order.

"Step up please, Canny man, an' receive your well-earned prize!"

"Hand-me-down-the Moon" McCann (he was 6 ft. 7^1/$_2$ in. when his socks were dry, which wasn't often) looked apprehensively at the table, fearing another envelope might make its appearance. But Seamus put his hand floorwards and into view came a parcel, about 3 ft. long by 2 ft. wide, which he placed carefully on the table.

"Whit the hell?" gasped Hand-me-down-the-Moon as he strode up. "Whut can this be?"

"Open it up! Show it tae the audience!" beamed Seamus. Canny's tentacle-like fingers soon made short work of the paper and in a matter of seconds the mysterious contents of the parcel were revealed to one and all - a large glass tank with a metal frame.

"Hey, whut's this? A'm no' wantin' tae keep goldfish. Whut fur huve ye got me this fish tank?"

"That, Canny ma boy, is a *minnow-trap*. It saves ye a lot o' bother catchin' mennins."

"Mennins? Whut wid A want wi' catchin' mennins? A might look kinda like a heron but that's as far as it gauns!"

Seamus was beginning to lose all patience. There was a limit to everyone's mental endurance:

"You use them for bait, ye stupit fool."

"Naw, *you* can use them for bait. Here, ye can have yer ain persunal mennin trap yersel!"

And, snatching it up, the elongated Canny banged it down on the table in front of Seamus. The noise was considerable as the tank - and one or two pieces of crockery - disintegrated.

"This is the stuff!" yelled Billy Howker delightedly. "Things is gettin' warmed up!"

Seamus did his best to compose himself, but the last vestige of his patience had now evaporated. His head went back and was then brought forward and down like a bullet to be planted plumb in the middle of Canny's protruding gut. There was a dull thump as the giant's overloaded digestive system had something further to complain about. And he received yet another thump as he collapsed over the table, taking trendy, over-cosmeticised Bessie Bisset with him. Bessie extracted her head from a full rhubarb bowl, one foot deep, and there was a peal of laughter from Billy Howker.

"At least that stuff'll wash off, Bessie. It's no' like that polyfilla below it. Whit dae you use tae get it off when ye get hame - a hammer and chisel?"

The mood had been set and scuffles, some strongly verbal, others mildly physical, began to break out all over the hall. The Darlin' Doonie and the more questionable Pauchle Puke were obviously beginning to take effect, and Seamus decided it would be sound strategy to channel his members' energies elsewhere. So, after intimating - amidst howls of protest - that there was no prize for the most sporting fisherman that year, simply because the club's coffers were about as dry as the Doonie had been throughout the entire summer, he gave orders for the dance to get under way, and the Doonieburnie Quarryblasters swung into raucous action with their unmelodious battery of pipes and accordions, saxophones and drums. It was a din that must have made the salmon in the nearby Doonie feel like fleeing back to the sea, but at least it curtailed most of the oral exchanges. There was no point in trying to compete with such a racket, so again physical strife tended to replace the verbal version.

Big Teenie McTavish, impatient to exercise those mighty limbs that would have done credit to a bull elephant, grabbed hold of Caw-Caw Candless. But Caw-Caw had had a real pailful of the crater and Teenie, from the look in his eye, deduced that he had intentions which might be neither strictly admirable nor to her moral well-being. These suspicions became near certainty when the 18-stone Queen of the Glen felt his grizzly cheek sandpaper her own. So Teenie lifted a massive knee.

Caw-Caw gave vent to a piercing scream and crawled off the floor.

His vowed state of permanent bachelorhood was, many reckoned, confirmed there and then.

Machine-Gun Massie, whose attempts at oral communication were reminiscent of a pneumatic drill with saliva flying off instead of sparks, was not slow to see the implications:

"Hey, C-C-Caw-Caw, that's pit an end t-t-t-tae yer gall-galliv-gallivantin' for a w-w-week or twa. It's the f-f-f-fireside fur you f-f-f-frae noo oan, c-c-c-cocky b-b-b-bendie."

Unfortunately, Dunkie Todd was standing directly in Machine-Gun's line of fire, which did nothing to enhance Dunkie's already rather woe-begone appearance. Using his neighbour's sleeve to get rid of this unwelcome and rather unsavoury spray, he entered into the spirit of things by pitching Machine-Gun head-first through the big drum just at the moment when its owner, Basher Bell, was bringing his stick down at rapid speed. Machine-Gun, his head protruding through the far side of the drum, received the wallop from the stick full on his ample posterior. The double roar of agony and his stuttered curses caused the spiders above to panic in their cobwebs and to think about weaving new homes elsewhere. But he soon recovered, crawled out of the other side of the drum and proceeded to send Basher sprawling on to the dance-floor with a butt that would have done a billy-goat proud.

One incident followed another, but when the hour moved round to two in the morning it was obvious that the Doonieburnians had spent themselves both physically and emotionally. And, like the tinkers up by the loch who fought like demons at night and were once again close-bosom friends in the morning, they retired from the scene of battle arm in arm, telling each other what a great night they had had. The digs and the innuendo and the scuffles and the thumps had been, were, and always would be the stuff of which the Doonieburnie Social was made, because it was one of the few remaining parts of the world where organised entertainment was practically unknown and fun was largely self-made. Excess steam had been let loose and the harsh tasks of the morrow would be that less onerous. The back-breaking toil in field and forest would be alleviated for some time by reference to the happenings at the Annual Social. Then, as the months passed, they would start smacking their lips in anticipation of the one to come. They knew it would take place, just as their much-loved Doonie and its tributary the Pauchle would keep on flowing, just as they would all be a year older. Whether they would be wiser as well would remain to be seen. But then, they were rough-hewn, endowed with a raw but innocent simplicity, and are there perhaps as a nostalgic reminder of a less sophisticated and more relaxed age which is now no more.

Double Bonus

EXCISE-OFFICER George Nimmo was the sort of person who saw little point in life if he could not fish. For him it was the only saving grace in an otherwise grey and rotten world.

With him the river took precedence over everything else that existed, coming before wife and family, home and garden and, very often, his job. Not that he failed to give these the consideration he knew they deserved. He did that all right, but if ever a conflict of loyalties arose, these were relegated to second place and received his undivided attention only when his appetite for rod and line had been sufficiently assuaged, which was not often.

And so he experienced nothing but despair when he was posted away from the first-class beat he had been fortunate enough to enjoy on Spey to take up office in a different part of the country. Not that in his new surroundings he wasn't within easy reach, mileage-wise, of excellent salmon water - a very fine stretch was but a quarter-of-an-hour's drive away. But unhappily permission was unattainable, which only served to increase his frustration as he plied a largely unproductive rod on a few tortured yards of association water. Feeling like a dethroned king, he pined for his former paradise on the lordly Spey, fretted, and was sad. In fact, at times his sadness bordered on melancholia.

Then, one morning, a small incident came as the first step towards the rekindling of the vital spark that had died low within him and was almost on the point of total extinction.

As he emerged from a shop in the local High Street, he was certain a passer-by had greeted him with a "Morning, Colonel!" He thought little more of it, but when practically the same thing happened as he left "The Salmon Leap" after a midday refreshment a couple of days later, he wondered just what was going on. Quickly he turned round to face the young man who had greeted him, and as he did so, he detected a slight air of puzzlement on the latter's countenance, followed by a hesitant: "It is you, isn't it, Colonel?"

George Nimmo had heard of Colonel Bainsford, the gruff, reticent owner of the famous Blackgordon Beat and, without quite knowing why but probably because his brain was working ahead of itself, he replied, not too affably, "Yes, morning!"

When the first opportunity presented itself he dressed up in casual but fairly orthodox clothes as might be worn by a country-lover - jerkin, polo neck and flannels - but he added sunglasses and hung about the wood bordering The Dead Pine, reputed to be the best pool of the entire Blackgordon Estate.

Eventually the Colonel arrived, parking his Range Rover on the rough track adjacent to this mecca of a salmon lie.

Nimmo's binoculars told him, or rather confirmed - and the experience was a strange one indeed - that Colonel Bainsford was in fact as near to being his own double as it was possible to imagine. The facial resemblance was almost uncanny. But the build as well, everything.

Methodical and painstaking by nature, Nimmo went back time and time again to his observation post - for that is exactly what it was - and noted, amongst smaller details, that the Colonel invariably wore the same tweed jacket, deerstalker and coarse shirt, either brown or maroon, without a tie, also green thigh waders, and that he wielded a 12 or $12^1/_2$ ft. fly rod very similar to his own.

Nimmo took himself off to the nearest large shopping centre and purchased, with no little difficulty, almost exact replicas of hat, shirt and jacket.

Then, one day shortly afterwards, he decided the time had come to take the plunge. Using the knowledge he had meticulously accrued over the weeks of observation, he made his way to the river, leaving his car in a lay-by well back on the main road and nearer to an adjoining beat than it was to Blackgordon. With slightly pounding heart he began to fish the topmost pool, since Colonel Bainsford obviously concentrated on the bottom end, and on The Dead Pine in particular.

The same pounding heart missed a beat or two when a small, stocky figure, whom he instantly recognised as the local bailiff, hailed him from the far bank:

"Have ye got a fush, Colonel?"

Nimmo, knowing that Bainsford was unpopular with many on account of his gruffness and uncommunicative temperament, shook his head, grunted simultaneously and went on with his casting. The bailiff, a frank, open character who found it difficult to cope with reticence, did not tarry and went on upstream.

Obviously, great care had to be exercised. For instance, if the water had risen the Colonel was apt to turn his attention to the pools at the upper extremity of the beat, so Nimmo always lay in wait until he could determine his whereabouts, then took himself off to what he considered to be the safest territory. Sometimes the Colonel did not appear at all, which usually indicated that he had had an extra heavy night with the gin bottle. Nimmo hoped that such orgies would become more frequent...

And so it went on, Nimmo enjoying, illegitimately and somewhat precariously, an angler's forbidden paradise. Certainly he had frights, such as on the morning when the same bailiff shouted across to him:

"By jove, Colonel, ye haven't been long getting here from The Pine! On foot at that! Ye must be very fit!"

On another occasion he remained casting well out in the water without

Tales of Fishing and Fishermen

advancing very far, as he was already in the tail of the pool, when once again the bailiff arrived, this time on Nimmo's side of the river. Praying for once that no salmon would take him, Nimmo kept his head low and his mouth shut and finally the bailiff, perturbed that a human being should be so wary of oral communication with his fellow man, went off with a sigh.

Nimmo caught fish, many fish, and had the luck of the devil in that he got off with his stratagem for so long. He was well aware that he was overstepping the mark and that he might well be inviting disaster, but danger, as we all know, has its excitements and its fascinations and, like the moth in the candle-flame, Nimmo had to accept that his days - or hours - or minutes - were inevitably numbered, it surely being only a matter of time before his wings were singed. Yet, as the weeks went by and his ruse remained undetected, he seemed to become more and more infected with the irrational belief characteristic of the habitually reckless motorist or the heavy smoker - it would never happen to him.

But happen it did, although in a manner he would never have suspected.

One morning, minutes after he had hooked a salmon obviously of the order of 30 lb, the river began to rise quickly following a prolonged and torrential downpour in the surrounding hills. Nimmo was well aware the Colonel would probably move upstream to take advantage of the extra water that always seemed to make The Oysters the best pool to fish, and accordingly he had to make a difficult choice. He had either to break his line and clear off while the going was good, or risk everything by trying to get the fish on to dry land as soon as possible. Tightening up his reel he pulled and hauled all he dared. It was a desperate situation.

After five minutes of what was more or less a tug-of-war, he had made little impression on the big salmon and he knew he had to make his mind up quickly. But it was too late.

He heard, then glimpsed out of the corner of his eye, an erratically-steered Range Rover. It stopped no more than a few yards away and out clambered the man with whom he had always feared a direct confrontation.

But Colonel Bainsford was still soaked with the previous evening's colossal intake of gin and lime, of which the greater part was gin. His doctor had constantly warned him that if he did not abstain, the hallucinations which had been afflicting him in ever-increasing intensity for months would finally mean hospitalisation, if not the madhouse.

For a moment he looked at Nimmo, nose twitching and hands trembling. Then his eyes rolled back in their sockets and he turned and ran, if that is the right word to describe his stumbling flight, emitting wild and unintelligible cries. Nimmo, bewildered and disconcerted, allowed the fish to tear off downstream and his 15lb line snapped like the flimsiest of thread.

132

Double Bonus

Finally convinced that his doctor had not been voicing idle threats, Bainsford never touched another drop and gradually regained his former robust health.

Nimmo, on recovering his composure after the extraordinary incident just related, remained apprehensive and puzzled by it, but not so disorientated that he did not realise the Colonel's extraordinary behaviour had let him off the hook, temporarily at least. He soon learned the truth about Bainsford's condition and, with the latter's return to good health, reluctantly accepted that his escapade was finished for ever, because the rejuvenated Colonel now pranced tirelessly and soberly up and down the entire beat.

So, having nothing to lose and even cherishing a slight hope that, in the circumstances, he might even profit from it, he donned different garb and approached the Colonel one fine autumn day. He explained, somewhat sheepishly, exactly what had happened. The other man listened, intrigued.

Bainsford was intelligent enough to realise right away that he probably owed Nimmo both his sanity and his life. And his appreciation was expressed in the form of a permit which allowed his double to fish, gratuitously, three of the pools two days every week - on the condition that while so doing he never wore a deerstalker or checked tweed jacket - and there was also a hint that he might like to get rid of his Army-type moustache.

The Obstruction

CAPTAIN JOHN SINCLAIR, Laird of Mellancraig and a man whose love of salmon fishing reached obsessive proportions, suddenly found himself beset by acute financial problems. These stemmed from a variety of causes, most of them of his own making.

A turkey-farmer on a large scale, Sinclair's sole hope of salvation, if his bank was to be appeased and a further breathing-space granted, lay in massive sales of birds for the Christmastide which was fast approaching. And he was confident of substantially reducing his crippling overdraft because his turkeys were big and plump and healthy. Orders from wholesalers were already pouring in, confirming press and TV reports that the nation at large was affected more than ever and earlier than usual, with the seasonal sickness of which the main symptom was an almost paranoic desire to rid itself of its silver. Anyone might have been excused for thinking that money, as a means of exchange, was about to become obsolete.

After strolling through some of the numerous pens and satisfying himself that all was in order, Sinclair still had half-an-hour to kill before lunch and decided to have a look at his own private stretch of the river. He expected a huge water after the unremitting deluge of the previous day.

He stopped and stared, then cursed loud and long. Although the season had ended weeks before, he thought immediately of his own spring fishing and how it could now be jeopardised - which was akin to saying that he would be an even unhappier man than he was. Such thoughts were provoked by the sight of a massive oak which had been torn from the bank a short distance upstream and now lay lodged with its branches groping skywards like long, disjointed arms, firmly stuck in what was the downmost and by far the best pool of his entire beat, The Ashes. It had come to rest right opposite the burn mouth, across the marvellous lie from which he - no lessee was ever allowed to fish there - had taken countless salmon over the years.

Sinclair cursed again, more vehemently, when he reached the spot and saw, from close quarters, the enormous size of the trunk and even of its branches. It was a job for a boat, the stoutest of chains and a heavy tractor, or rather it would have been, if access for the latter had been possible, which it was not. Such was the nature of the surrounding terrain that no machine could have got anywhere near the place. Nothing short of a helicopter could have tackled the obstruction - to him, in his present state, a financially impracticable solution - and he gained some sort of negative solace from the fact that there was probably no type in the country, if indeed in existence, powerful enough to budge that huge tree, let alone lift it.

He considered other methods. Explosives? Impossible until the low waters of summer, by which time the spring run would have gone through

unmolested and salmon fishing was usually not worth bothering about. But there had to be a way, because he simply could not miss out on that wonderful pool during those first few exciting weeks of the coming season, commencing on January 15. Compared to them, the rest of the year paled into insignificance.

But Sinclair, on reflection, became slightly more optimistic. Perhaps another colossal flood would coax the tree out of the lie, especially if a dam of debris was formed, thereby increasing the pressure of the water pushing against it; but in all probability this was a forlorn hope.

A forlorn hope indeed. Twenty hours of torrential rain and a 12 ft. rise failed to move the tree an inch. A heavy branch must have become trapped amongst big boulders and if that gigantic wall of water, driving relentlessly forward as only water can, couldn't shift the oak, what could?

Sinclair now saw only one possibility, one which might well solve the problem, but could just as easily aggravate it. He waited for the next big spate - it came early in December - and had some of his estate hands fell an even larger oak which grew just above the former site of the one now spoiling the pool. He reckoned that at least one of its great boughs would dig deep towards the river-bottom and, bolstered by the force of the current and the solid weight of the trunk, would lever the culprit out of that place where it had no right to be and that both trees would float off together downstream. Which they did.

Locked together in a giant embrace, like two huge octopuses wrestling to the death as they revolved and pirouetted in a weird, aquatic dance, amidst the cracking and snapping of their smaller branches, they pitched and tossed and trundled their way out of Sinclair's pool, out of Sinclair's beat, no doubt to go and bother someone else. The Laird allowed himself a rare smile, pulled up his collar against the first flakes of the winter's snow, and departed when he saw them disappear round the broad bend which marked the beginning of his neighbour's water.

So he failed to see them accelerate down through the narrow stream called The Sluice and head towards the central pillar of the road bridge. The century-old structure, forbidden to vehicles over a certain tonnage and earmarked by the Regional Council for imminent repair, was dealt a sudden *coup de grâce* because, doughty victor of many assaults as it had been, this was a monumental force with the like of which it could no longer cope. It shuddered as if in agony and the middle 30 ft. fell into the river.

It snowed and it snowed. Eight inches... twelve... fifteen... with incredible drifts billowing out of a silent, white wilderness. Then came a vicious frost, which went on and on. Christmas was approaching and Sinclair's turkeys were due to be despatched for what was an insatiable market. In more normal circumstances he could have got his staff to clear the road for his vans, difficult as this would have been, as the local railway station stood only a mile away - but on the other side of the river. With the bridge down the shortest detour was one of over 30 miles along minor hill roads, and such a journey was hopelessly out of the question.

So Christmas came and went and the turkeys stayed where they were.

Ironic, mused Sinclair. The Ashes, cleared of its obstruction, would be holding a shoal of springers within a few weeks. But who would be catching them?

Two Men in a Boat

BOB KELLY and Sandy Baird were in despair. The private estate of Gorlie, where, by virtue of favours rendered to an appreciative and amiable laird, they had been fortunate enough to fish for years, had been sold, and no permits were being issued to any of the local anglers. The favoured few would all be big business associates of the new owner, or "social celebrities" from the South, who would be invited up to fish when expediency so demanded.

Bob and Sandy made every effort to obtain permission elsewhere, but without success. As spring passed into summer and the sea trout came storming up from the estuary, they were almost at their wits' end.

It was one evening in early June that Sandy got his idea. As the two friends stood on the bridge watching the water, which was a poor substitute for plying it with rod and line, two or three canoes came gliding downstream.

"Ye ken, Bob, I've heard it said that naebody can stop ye gaun doon the water in a boat. It's getting access tae the river that's the trouble. Noo, that path doon there is public an' if ye launched a boat here, you could sail right doon through a' that private water, through Gorlie an' Tundarrock an' Rostocan an' Balmain an' then bring the boat ashore on the estuary. Naebody could say a word."

"But it's fishin' we want, no sailin'. What guid is that tae us?"

"Ye no' see man? Rods in the bottom o' the boat. Cruise slowly doon the flats in the dark an' fish. It would be great, man. We just sit oan oor backsides an' fish away. If oanybody offers oany trouble, we'll just row into deep water till we get the rods doon an' hide them under some auld sheets we'll pit in the boat. Then we're in the clear. Mebbe ye can even fish legally frae a boat, I dinnae ken, but if ye cannae we can manage it the way I said."

Bob agreed it was well worth a try. It seemed a possible solution to all their problems. Only one thing worried him as far as the execution of the plan was concerned. Once they got down to the estuary, how were they to get the boat back six miles upstream to the bridge? But Sandy had thought of that as well.

"We'll just have to get a trailer fur it, an' we're lucky baith oor caurs are rigged up fur that already. An' if we use baith o' them there'll be nae bother. Suppose I drive ma caur doon tae the estuary an' you follow me wi' yours wi' the boat hitched tae it. I leave ma caur doon there an' you tak' us up tae the brig wi' the boat. You leave your caur there an' when we've fished right doon the river we'll have ma caur waitin' fur us tae tak' us an' the boat back hame. Then I'll tak' ye up fur your caur so ye can drive it back. Then the next time we gaun fishin' we just dae much the same wi' me drivin' us an' the boat up tae the brig after I've come wi' ye doon tae the estuary wi' your caur so that it will be there fur us tae get hame wi' the boat. You tak' the boat hame an' me up tae the brig fur ma caur. Then I follow you back. S'easy!"

"Easy? Soons a bit complicated tae me." Bob wondered if the Allied Invasion of Europe in 1944 could have been as detailed either in its planning or its execution.

Without being too sure of the legal position, because there were so many conflicting beliefs on such matters amongst the angling fraternity, Sandy knew there was a definite advantage in the law-breaker being one step ahead of the law-maker. So even if they were stopped and investigated, there would be no precedent to follow and there should be nothing to worry about in that respect. Only that their game, which seemed so promising, might be brought to an abrupt end if the Courts decided it was definitely agin the law of the land. But such cases usually ended up with admonishment.

After some reflection, Bob asked:

"What aboot gettin' the boat through the rough bits whar there's rocks an' things? They'll tear the erse oot o' it!"

"Naw, we'll keep clear o' rocks, dinnae worry!" answered Sandy, perhaps with less conviction than Bob would have desired.

A boat was duly procured from an old yard down on the coast, at a price so inviting that they wondered about its river-worthiness. But a close inspection, which included the odd clout with a hob-nailed boot, failed to reveal any weakness, either through damp rot, dry rot, or any other known form of rot. And so it was bought, together with a trailer, and the firm of Kelly and Baird was equipped and ready for business.

They decided the first foray would take place on the Friday, and by the time it was half-dark, they were afloat, gliding silently, slowly, down the first long flat, then into the rapids of the next pool. Then more quiet water.

"Whit the bloody hell!" came a shout from an irate angler who, wading well out in breasters, was almost up-ended by the silent wooden monster which so unexpectedly had come looming upon him out of the failing light.

Then on the next flat:

"Gad! What in God's name are you doing out there in that thing, damn you! Don't you know this is private water?" They were now on the bottom beat of Gorlie and its new owner was known as a toffee-nosed individual of the least tolerant kind. Bob and Sandy ducked as low as they could and willed the boat to pick up speed, which it didn't, and it seemed an age before they were in the cant and accelerating into the next pool, where they received an even worse reception, having to face a barrage, not only of words, but of stones. They were fast beginning to wonder if they had been so clever after all. They still had not cast a line.

Two Men in a Boat

They had just reached the habitually quiet waters of Rostocan and felt they could settle to the purpose for which they were there.

Both had their rods in their hands and were peeling line off their reels for the first cast when it happened. The old boat, which had taken one or two knocks on its downstream journey and whose structural defects had been concealed beneath liberal coatings of tar, creosote and paint, scraped against a sharp underwater obstacle. It split all the way along the main seam and broke into two parts.

Bob and Sandy hauled themselves from the water. All their tackle was lost in the dark depths.

Utterly deflated, they made their way across the estate to the main road. Yapping dogs brought out owner and gillie and keeper, and they were challenged and held.

The dripping pair were escorted into a gun-room and, when their story was told, a laird who had a rare sense of humour and was a bit of a rebel himself, did not seem to be too annoyed over their abortive attempt to get some fishing. He was addicted to the sport himself and not so selfish as to be completely unsympathetic. Not that he gave them the slightest hint of his intentions.

They were ordered to come back the next day, wondered why, and feared the worst. But they were told to lead the way to the spot where they had capsized and, from a boat which was river-worthy, their tackle was eventually found and recovered. Then they were each handed a piece of paper stating they had permission to fish Rostocan between 6 pm and midnight on Tuesdays and Thursdays from the first day of June until the end of September. You could have floored them with one of the wisps of feathers with which they made their flies.

They learned later that the Laird of Rostocan was a man who admired initiative and that their escapade had reminded him of the occasions on which two other men, of whom he was one, had crept stealthily at dead of night in a midget submarine into places where they had no right to be (Norwegian fjords, for example) in order to put one over on others who wanted to rule the roost.

Perhaps that had something to do with it.

The Inseparables

Bachelors Danny Finlayson and Frank Mercer had been friends since their early schooldays - if "friends" be the right word, for theirs was the type of relationship, almost religious in its fervour, which was cemented by unbreakable bonds. It was a liaison so deep and of such selfless intensity as to be quite rare amongst humans anywhere. Born perhaps of mutual disaster - they had both lost their fathers in the same accident - their closeness had grown as they had served together in North Africa, and when Danny was captured by one of Rommel's panzer divisions, Frank had appeared in the same prison camp not long after. They had escaped together, rejoined their unit, and fought side by side right through Sicily and up through Italy. Then, the war over, they had returned to their West Highland village and bought a small cottage which they shared. Frank had been employed at the hydro-electric plant and Danny on the farm not half-a-mile distant.

Then had come that awful May morning when slight, red-haired Frank, at work on the sluice gates, had simply disappeared without trace. The police had dragged every pool right down to the sea, but without success.

Danny, heartbroken, shut himself off from the world for days on end.

Five or six weeks passed before others genuinely interested in his welfare managed to persuade him that the yawning vacuum might be partially filled, and the pain lessened if he started fishing again, as this had been the most important thing in his life after Frank. To help tempt him, he was told of a marvellous run of fish and one or two "monsters" which had been seen going over the falls near the village. Their arguments finally won him over when he was reminded that he would be participating in the pastime he and Frank had enjoyed so much together, and that he might feel himself a little nearer his departed friend. Frank would not be far away.

So one June morning he checked his tackle, which in happier days had never lain unused for very long, and made his way to the best holding pool on the stretch, named the Black Bluidy Hole.

It was an awesome place. A safe sanctuary for ascending salmon during spells of drought, it was flanked on the far side by a dark, forbidding overhang towering upwards for more than a 100 ft., with beads of greenish water continually dripping from it. The top of the Bluidy was extremely narrow and through this channel poured the entire flow of the river, so that even during low conditions the thunderous roar and the reverberations from the overhang made it a place not too suitable for those of nervous disposition. The right bank alone provided a modicum of accessibility, since it had several shelves of slippery rock, the lowest some ten feet above a churning whirlpool which knocked a three-inch minnow about as if the latter had come to life and gone crazy. If a fish was hooked from this position - and the Bluidy could be tackled from no other spot - it was just possible, if you were as sure of foot as a mountain goat and as nerveless as a lion, to work your way down to the tail where Nature, perhaps regretting somewhat the fearsome contours and the general air of foreboding with which she had invested this place, had relented enough to provide a small, welcoming spit of gravel where a salmon could be landed in low water.

It almost goes without saying, that in spite of its potentiality, most anglers avoided the Bluidy altogether, preferring to fish in less awesome, if also less productive, surroundings.

Plying a rod there had never unduly bothered either Danny or Frank, probably because they had been accustomed to it from quite a tender age, when they had known no fear and had but few inhibitions. The Black Bluidy Hole had yielded them many a fine salmon, and it was to it that Danny directed his steps, albeit hesitatingly, that Saturday morning in June.

He edged his way forward to the casting shelf and threw his minnow to the foot of the overhang opposite. Then his thoughts turned to Frank and the mysterious nature of his going, and he retrieved his lure rather more quickly than usual.

He also became more conscious of the great dark rock face opposite him and of the turbulent, roaring water, which was steadily increasing in volume as the sluice gates had been opened not many moments before. After his third cast, he manoeuvred his feet to make certain he had the safest possible stance. He kept casting with determination, assuring himself it was pleasant to be back enjoying his old pursuit, yet he was possessed of a vague, uncomfortable feeling, and was half-hoping that no salmon would show any interest in his Devon. As the latter was drawn and pulled about by the powerful currents that were darkly at work in that bottomless pit, his eye followed the track he himself would have to follow to deal with a fish - and the prospect appalled him.

Then his minnow stopped and he tightened instinctively. His quarry seemed to wish to keep well down, as all salmon were wont to do in that great seething cauldron of a place. As he put on pressure, it came with him, then seemed to surrender itself to the pull of the various currents. This was how monster salmon usually behaved in the Black Bluidy Hole.

Danny's line was now almost vertically beneath him and he put on more strain in case his quarry let itself be sucked further into the whirlpool and his line broken by the resultant pressure. So he heaved, steady and hard. It came up slowly...

Danny saw matted red hair and a ghastly countenance. Frenzied, his ear-piercing scream was cut short as he fell forward to shatter his head on a protruding rock and land alongside his much-lamented friend.

The Day the Cranes came

It WAS quite an appealing sort of letter and amusing as well, the type that makes a refusal difficult. It came from a club in North Yorkshire, calling itself "The Cranes", and asked for a day - just one day - for 14 of its members on our Border loch. The club had one or two miles of weed-choked canals and a little stretch of river, or what had once been a river, because, according to the writer, it was "red one day, green the next, then a dazzling blue that put the Mediterranean to shame. Then sometimes it is a mixture of all three. Strangers look skywards, expecting to see the rainbow of rainbows but we locals just smile, knowing they are working overtime in the dyeworks". The Second World War was not long over and many of England's rivers were still in an awful state, no less than open sewers.

And so, as a magnanimous gesture of the brotherhood that exists amongst all exponents of the so-called gentle art, our committee granted the request. Perhaps it should be whispered that the £30 offered by the Yorkshiremen might have helped towards this decision, because our funds were low and we needed money for restocking. Also, we were not unaware of the fact that our visitors, coarse fishing addicts to a man, could do us further good by ridding the loch of some of the pike and perch which were becoming far too numerous.

Our sleeping village was duly awakened shortly after 8 a.m. on a Saturday in July, when a rickety old bus rattled a swerving course along the main street. Goodness knows when they had left home, but the stalwarts from Yorkshire had been offered a full day and a full day they intended to have.

Angus McCaddem, our secretary, had arranged to meet the coach and guide it to the water. This he did in his usual helpful manner.

He left the visitors just after half-past-eight, as soon as the bus had been parked on a grassy strip near the head of the loch. But before setting off for home on his old motor-cycle, he stared in amazement at the amount and variety of gear being removed from their conveyance. It formed a veritable mountain of great thick rods, rod rests, huge creels, picnic baskets, oil stoves, folding stools, keep-nets, tins of groundbait, jars of bread paste, cheese paste, fish paste and probably every other paste ever concocted, thermometers, sets of scales and many other unrecognisable gadgets - and, handled more carefully than anything else, several huge crates of beer. Angus decided he had better return later in the day - our beloved loch had been polluted once before and it was a problem which had caused no end of trouble before it was finally resolved.

He came back at one o'clock with Don Candlish, a knowledgeable trout angler and a useful committee member for over 20 years. Little did the two suspect that they were about to witness the most nightmarish phantasmagoria that could ever take place on a fishing expedition.

When they emerged from a group of trees to come upon one of the sheltered inlets, they were confronted with a fiendish hissing sound and an urgent flapping of wings as the surface of the water erupted in foam and spray. Wiry little Joe Tunstall was holding on to his rod in bewilderment as a hefty mute swan scudded across the bay in an attempt to become airborne, tearing yards of nylon from his singing reel. Unfortunately, it headed straight for the spot where Wilf Puddlethwaite was stretched out on a ridge of soft sand amidst a wealth of empties, his great round gut heaving up and down like a buoy in a storm-tossed sea while he emitted strident whistles of such intensity as to increase the not inconsiderable terror already being experienced by the swan. The latter, now panic-stricken and still only airborne a few inches, realised it was on a collision course with an obviously strange and solid obstacle and swerved violently upwards and to the right. As the great bird passed overhead, the nylon dragged under Wilf's left foot, tightened, and was drawn up his leg to catapult him unceremoniously head-over-heels and plant him in the loch with a resounding splash. He struggled out, gave himself a good shake and reached for another bottle of beer.

Meanwhile, Joe's reel emptied and the nylon parted with a resounding crack. The swan, trailing several yards of heavy monofilament and with a four-inch spoon impaled on its hindquarters, went off as if jet-propelled to escape this mad circus which had descended on its normally peaceful haunts, to seek out a more tranquil stretch of water somewhere to the north. Fortunately the sudden jerk had loosened the hooks, and the spoon and the nylon, together with a few feathers, fell into the loch.

When the commotion had died down completely and Wilf, once adequately restocked with liquid fuel, was endeavouring to light a fire to dry off some of his sodden clothes, Angus and Don continued their walk, their faces expressing a mixture of disbelief and amusement, tinged with apprehension.

They had neither far to go nor long to wait before coming upon the second act of this unexpected loch-side comedy. The long and sinewy Herbert Featherstall was about to heave an enormous ball of pink paste far out into the ripples, but as he swung his rod behind him for the forward cast, his finger slipped from the spool and the spherical offering went flying back to catch his portly companion, Charlie Pickup, at that precise moment draining the last potent dregs from an outsize bottle of ale, such a thumping blow on the back of the cranium that his whole face was pushed forwards and three or four of his new National Health dentures smashed against the thick glass around which his chubby lips were compressed. The whole mouthful - plastic teeth, fragments of red gum and a good draught of dark brown beer were ejected with explosive force right into the dead-pan countenance of Big Bob Blower, who had chosen that exact moment to come along and ask Charlie if he had any ale to spare.

By this time Angus and Don thought no more such scenes were possible. But they were wrong. When they rounded the next headland, they saw one of the association's boats drifting along a few yards offshore with one-legged Turkey Trafford lying propped across the bows, casting away with a light fly rod, but with his trouser leg wound right to the top of his peg to which was attached, by means of leather straps, what must have been the prototype of the first ever spinning-reel. Huge rod rings could be distinguished at short intervals along the timber, and Turkey was using his ingenious contraption to trawl worm with his left leg while he fished fly with his right arm.

The next thing to arrest their attention was the sudden pealing of a very loud bell and they hurried round a an outcrop of rocks jutting out into the loch to witness yet another riveting scene before them.

Tommy Todkill had been fast asleep, sheltered by an awning he had erected because of the coolish breeze, when the metal bell fixed near his rodtip had begun, in no uncertain manner, to fulfil the purpose for which it was there. They saw him jump to his feet, grab his butt and start to play a pike bigger than any they had even feared the water might hold.

But they had never seen a fish played like this before. Tommy simply applied the screw and instead of pumping the pike, he walked backwards up the hillside, dragging his quarry nearer the bank. Unfortunately, he stepped on to an over-ripe tomato sandwich discarded by a fellow Crane and his rod went flying from his grasp to be promptly jerked waterwards by the monster he had hooked. His friend, Albert Leatherbottom, saw the danger and made a dive at the butt as it was about to disappear into the depths of the loch, but he was a fraction too late and when he picked his face out of the water it was coated in a glorious mixture of stagnant watercress and mature frog spawn.

Around three o'clock, it was obvious that a violent thunderstorm was fast approaching from the west and the visitors, acting normally for once, gathered up their various pieces of equipment and made a bee-line for the coach. Angus and Don hurriedly pulled on their capes and headed for the club hut, but halted in their tracks as they caught sight of poor Dickie Tuff, who had never got the hang of these "new-fangled" reels as he called them. Dickie was hopelessly entwined in the biggest bird's nest of all time. The line was even tangled round his legs and this made him so immobile that he could do nothing but stand there and fume and curse and shout for help as huge pellets of hail bounced off his hairless scalp like so many ping-pong balls.

The storm moved away to the east and when Angus and Don returned to the loch later with some of the other local anglers who were dubious about what they had heard and wanted to see for themselves, the curtain had come down on the final act and the invaders had beaten a reluctant retreat. Not that they had departed without leaving ample evidence of their visit, because there were enough cans and beer bottles strewn around to fill a good-sized truck while sheep, cattle and seagulls were busy scavenging the surrounding turf and shingle for the remnants of pork pies, cold sausages, egg and tomato sandwiches and goodness knows what other titbits of doubtful ingredients. And all the time a lonely swan floated miserably up and down the loch, bewildered by the day's happenings and wondering why his mate had indulged in such extraordinary behaviour and where on earth she had gone.

Incident on the A837

ROGER ALLERTON cruised out of the hotel drive near the Sutherland village of Lochinver and pointed his Jaguar in the general direction of London.

He was not feeling too pleased, either with himself or with the world at large. After a week on one of the choicest rivers of the entire North, which is saying something, he had not a single fin to take back South for the dinner party he and his wife were giving a couple of days later, which is also saying something, because, before his departure, he had boasted to his executive friends, some of them anglers themselves, about his prowess with a salmon rod and had promised they would partake of a succulent steak practically as soon as he got back. He had tried to buy a fish, but couldn't. The North was packed out with tourists, British and foreign, and salmon, which they could seldom enjoy elsewhere, was on nearly every hotel menu - and the price did not deter them. Hence the scarcity.

"Damn it all!" said Allerton out loud. "What can I do?" He had even been tempted, on his last outing the previous day, to sink his hooks into an unsuspecting salmon he had spied lying beside a rock ledge. Only the fear of being caught, and the ignominy which would result therefrom, had dissuaded him from taking such a drastic step.

A few miles further on his thoughts were interrupted by the sight of a figure frantically gesticulating to him to stop. "Well," he thought, "there are few queeries up here. Should be safe enough."

He began to wonder if he had done the right thing when he got a closer view of the man: torn gumboots, a filthy coat which was half-a-dozen sizes too big for him, moth-eaten cap, and facial features which suggested that so far fate had not treated him too kindly. But it was too late, for a gnarled hand had already opened the door and Allerton had a passenger.

"Thank ye, thank ye, sur. A'm gaun doon tae Bonar Brig. It's awfu' kind o' ye."

"Not at all."

"Are ye gaun far, sur?"

"Yes, to London."

"Tae London, eh? That's a long road. Ye'll no' get there the nicht even wi' this motor?"

"No, I'll stop off for the night somewhere in the south of Scotland or Cumbria."

"Huve ye been oan yer hoalidays?"

"Yes."

"Been fishin'?"

"Yes."

"Oany luck?"

"No."

"Ye mean ye got nothin', nothin' at a'?"

"I got nothing, nothing at all!"

"An' so yer gaun back tae London withoot a fush?"

"Yes, I'm afraid so."

"Man, that's a pity, a great pity." More than you're aware, my man, thought Allerton. But he didn't bother to explain.

"Did ye no' want tae tak' a fush back wi' ye tae show off tae yer freends doon there?"

"Of course I bloody well did!" The question was just too pertinent.

"Weel noo, whit a shame, whit a richt shame!"

A few moments silence followed, and Allerton began to feel he had no right to treat his guest, such as he was, with such reticence. It served little purpose to vent his ill-temper on some poor Highland soul who had no conception of the niceties of life and who looked as if he had to struggle hard merely to stay alive. He ought to be more affable. Anyway, a bit of conversation, no matter on what level, would help to shorten the first few miles of the journey.

"What's your line of business?" he asked, trying to sound truly interested, although he had already decided that such a down-at-heel creature could have no "line of business" as such.

"Weel noo, that's kinda difficult tae explain. Let's say A jist dander aboot tryin' tae see whit's in the offin'. If ye keep yer eyes open an' tak' a' the chances that come yer way it's surprisin' hoo ye can get oan. Or get by..." The last statement seemed to be added as an afterthought, as if the one preceding it needed some modification.

Allerton, understandably, did not understand. He had heard of canny Highlanders before. This one could well be the archetype.

Again, silence for a minute or two, then:

"A could get ye a fush."

"You could? You know someone who would sell me one?"

"Naw, A dinnae, but jist stop at the next bend an' pit yer motor oan the grass."

Allerton was puzzled, but complied nevertheless.

"Noo, sur, jist you wait here. A'll no' be mony meenits. Peep yer horn if ye see oanybody comin'."

Allerton remained in the car. He saw his abettor take a good look around, then make his way down to the water's edge, extracting a length of wire from a spacious coat pocket as he did so. His coat was thrown off on to the bank, followed by trousers and jacket. The man now wore nothing but a pair of swimming trunks and the wire which was coiled round his neck. He clambered out over some rocks and swam out to a big one sticking up in midstream. Allerton saw him peer into the smooth patch of water in the lee of the rock, brace himself, then lower the noose. About ten seconds later it was jerked upwards and as the Sutherlander held firmly on to the rock with one hand, a splendid fish of about 12 lb. threw itself into the air. Allerton could already see it as the *pièce de résistance* at the dinner party. What would he say he took it on? A Jock Scott? A Silver Wilkinson? No, he would give the credit to a fly of his own making. That would sound even more impressive.

The man hung on grimly to both rock and fish until the latter gave up a struggle it was bound to lose. He swam to the edge, dragging the salmon with him. Then clobbered it with a stone as soon as he had it on dry land.

Allerton had stared at the whole operation, entranced, only diverting his eyes now and again to scan the road in both directions, just in case. He felt quite elated, perhaps no less over the man's skill than the fact that he had a salmon to take home. Convinced there was no other living soul within miles, he jumped out of the car and opened the boot as his saviour came forward with the booty.

"Now then!"

The words came from a tall, burly figure who had appeared from behind a big rock.

Allerton's elation, in the space of a fraction of a second, became sheer despair. The voice was like a voice from hell, damning him, because he was an accomplice, as much involved as the Sutherlander. He, Roger Allerton, company chairman and renowned and respected industrialist, stood there holding the boot open to receive the fish. He turned round, his face already ashen, to see he was confronted by a man who was obviously a water bailiff. God, he was a common criminal! How could he have been so utterly stupid? And all out of sheer vanity. Nothing else.

The bailiff took the fish and put it in his own boot, then noted down Allerton's name and address and car number. He already knew all details pertaining to the Sutherlander, having tangled with him on more than one occasion. Intimating that they would hear from the Authorities in due course, he departed, satisfied that this incident would prove once more to his superiors that he was a loyal and responsible servant.

"I should leave you here and let you walk to Bonar Bridge," said Allerton. "A nice pickle of fish you've landed me in" - in different circumstances he might have appreciated his own pun - and then added: "And yourself as well, although it perhaps doesn't mean as much to you. But I suppose you might as well get back into the car."

After they had gone a mile or so, during which time his passenger seemed to be concentrating on a letter he had taken from an inside pocket, Allerton, his mind in a turmoil, broke the silence:

"Well, my man, have you nothing to say?"

"Whit aboot?"

"Oh, don't be so damned annoying! You know very well what I mean. Here I am, a dedicated salmon angler, an all-fly man, a renowned purist, and I'll have to come back up to Lairg or some God-forsaken place to answer a poaching charge, details of which will no doubt find their way into the national press. That's what it's about!"

"Weel, A'm no' worried!"

"You're not worried? But you're even more guilty than I am. You were the real culprit. If I hadn't given you a lift, this wouldn't have happened. What do you mean you're not worried? You'll be appearing in court at the same time as me."

"No, A'll no'. Nur you aither."

"Oh, for God's sake, man, talk some sense. What's got into you?"

"Weel, ye ken, A did tell ye A tak' a' the chances that come ma way, did A no' noo? Tak' a look at this!"

"What is it?"

"Ye didnae see me pickin' up this envelope when that big bastard o' a baillie pood it oot o' his pocket wi' his wee book? An' dropped it?"

"No, I didn't."

"A'm no' surprised. A wiz quick tae cover it up wi' ma fit."

"Well, what about it?"

"Jist that it's a letter frae a fishmonger in Inverness tae that big baillie tellin' him he wants nae mair salmon frae him because the last lot had been pishoned wi' cymag. We're in the clear, sur. If ye stop at the next 'phone box - there's yin twa or three miles doon the road - A'll speak tae that snifflin' swindlin' bugger. He'll be at hame fur his denner by noo."

Allerton, confused but glimpsing some possible hint of salvation, did as requested, and the Sutherlander returned to the car with a triumphant sneer on his face:

"That's fixed him. An' A telt him we wiz gaun richt back tae his hoose tae get that fish. He says it'll be in a bag under the bush at the front gate. An' A telt him tae that A'll jist hold oan tae this letter. It's like huvin' a permit tae poach." And he rubbed his hands together gleefully.

The dinner party was enjoyed by all, not least by Allerton.

One more "Ticket"

ACCORDING to many of the local residents, and especially the estate workers, gamekeeper Hugh McAllister had always been a wily one. It was whispered that he had sometimes trapped and sold the game he was paid to protect, whether it ran or flew or swam. But he had never gone over the score, keeping his transgressions within reasonable bounds and using the money to buy little luxuries that his relatively low wages would have prevented him from acquiring in any other way.

Then, when he retired, a benevolent Laird, quite ignorant of his servant's past misdemeanours, compensated him for his many years in his employment by allowing him to stay on rent-free in the Lodge and giving him the undemanding job of selling tickets for the water which he was now letting on a daily basis at a cost of £15. There was no wage, but he received 50 pence commission on each ticket sold. So, with his pension, his vast vegetable garden and orchard, with his bees and his chickens and his breeding-kennels with their periodic litters of fine Scotch terrier pups, he and his wife were comfortably off financially. And the life was peaceful, almost idyllic.

In the early-summer/early-autumn period, when holiday anglers were always searching for water, the stretch (not a particularly choice one compared with other beats of the river, mainly because it was overfished, although some individuals struck it lucky now and again with up to five fish for their day) was usually fully booked, which meant that 12 tickets were sold, most of them one or two days in advance. McAllister was not slow to notice that on any given day usually only 10 or 11 of the 12 ticket-holders turned up - illness, hangovers, sudden business commitments, nagging wives were some of the reasons - and decided he might as well try, literally, to cash in on the situation. Even if 13 and not 12 anglers were scattered about the water, who would notice? And no one ever seemed to check what was going on.

He managed to bribe his nephew, who worked for a firm of printers in Dundee, to produce for him a book of permits identical to those used on the estate, but with some of the writing and all the numbers smudged sufficiently to make the latter more or less indecipherable, if not completely illegible.

Once the 12 legitimate tickets had been sold, the crafty McAllister began, in high summer, to issue an extra one or two per day of the smudged variety from the faked book, thus pocketing between £126 and £216 every week, including his commission. And soon he became so sure of himself, and so money-crazy, that he considered it a great pity that he didn't get the 50 pence commission on the counterfeit permits as well.

His bank balance grew. And he would, of an evening, sit and stare at the figures as if entranced, when normally he would have been seeing to his bees or his chickens or his tomatoes or his new-born pups. The previously immaculate garden and its surrounds fell into a state of neglect. But he seemed hardly to notice, and certainly didn't care. Money had become his new God.

Becoming ever bolder in working what he thought was a perfect scheme, a day arrived when he sold not one, or two, or even three, but five tickets over the limit.

It was also a day which witnessed one of those combinations of fatal factors which now and again unveil the hitherto undiscovered and unsuspected. For one thing all 12 anglers were on the water. And the Laird himself, having been advised by his doctor to spend less time in the office and more around the estate, preferably on foot, decided to do just that and have a long-overdue look at the river. He walked along the entire stretch, chatting to some of the anglers and, at the end of it all, getting the impression that there were more than 12 people fishing. Still more out of curiosity than anything else, he retraced his steps, asking each of them to produce his permit and counting the total number. It was 17. A closer examination of the pieces of paper showed how the ploy had been worked.

One more piece of paper remained to be issued, this time by the Laird himself. Made out in the name of Hugh McAllister.

Wee Charlie

WEE CHARLIE was used to seeing affluence, although that was about as near to it as he ever got. The 11-year-old son of a woodman whose cottage stood a mile or two outside a popular Highland tourist centre, he could not help notice, during the summer, the superabundance of costly items of equipment of every conceivable kind which were flaunted by the holiday-makers flooding into the area. Whether it was for fishing, climbing, sailing or whatever, they seemed to have everything - and more besides. Some items he couldn't even identify, and they remained a mystery to him.

In the absence of such materialism his own forms of recreation were largely self-made. But he enjoyed it that way, deriving from his own efforts a delight unknown to many of the pampered offspring of well-heeled parents who, in spite of their expensive playthings, or perhaps because of them, were spoiled, easily dissatisfied and even basically unhappy.

Wee Charlie loved fishing. At every opportunity he grabbed his old greenheart, bequeathed by a much-loved grandfather, jumped astride his bike, (bought with money earned from odd little jobs on the estate), and headed for the not-too-distant burn. It wasn't big as burns go, but it was a wild water, characterised by deep pools, and contained the occasional trout of over the 1 lb. mark. But, perhaps more than most streams in the neighbourhood, it had to be known intimately. There were places where the trout were few and far between, others where they were quite plentiful but reluctant to take; and again there were spots where they were both prolific and often hungry. Charlie knew just where to go, which size and type of worm was best, and how to present it for maximum effect. He was a grand wee fisher, and if he returned with nothing for the tea-table, then it was highly unlikely that other households were partaking of fresh rod-caught trout that same evening.

When June came along one year recently, it brought with it the ever-growing spate of tourists who filled all the hotels and guest-houses - and the rich salmon beats of the big river. But there was one, a certain Mr. Geoffrey Whittaker, who denounced salmon fishing as an entirely hit-or-miss business requiring little skill on the part of the angler, where success depended wholly on the whim of the fish, whereas the brownie, even if in dour mood, could be persuaded to take - if you were an expert like himself. According to him, he had won many a contest in the South, both on still waters and on the chalk streams and was, in that region, and even furth of it, an acknowledged expert on flies and nymphs and lines and shooting-heads and on anything at all pertaining to *salmo trutta* and the purist approach. And so confident was he of his prowess that he perhaps did a little more bragging on his first day in the hotel than was wise, promising those guests who were too polite to turn away from his eternal chatter that, if they wished, they would have fresh trout for breakfast every morning throughout his stay.

But after five days and with only one to go, he was almost frantic, having taken only a handful of rather puny fish and too well aware that his self-sung reputation as a doyen amongst the troutmen was suffering by the hour. Then he was really at his wits' end with embarrassment when one of the guests, one of those "hit-or-miss" salmon men, laid out a fresh-run 10-pounder on the slab in the vestibule, for all to see - and eat. The gasps of admiration overheard by Whittaker were like so many kicks in the teeth, and literally made him feel sick. He just had to get those trout on his last day. Otherwise breakfast on the final morning would be one hellish torment.

He had been advised by one of the tip-conscious hotel staff to try a little-known burn which no one seemed to bother about. He was also informed of the best points of access and how to reach them.

He was just parking his big hatchback on a patch of grass beside the stile and path leading to forest and burn when Wee Charlie arrived on his bike from the opposite direction.

Mr. Whittaker stared at Charlie's rod and meagre equipment with a mixture of pity and derision, but mainly derision. Couldn't his parents have fitted him out better than that? (Whittaker's own boys had everything even remotely connected with the hobbies they pursued). What chance could such a mite possibly have with such poor gear? Or anyone for that matter?

He decided to have word with him. He couldn't resist making an impression, even on a young boy:

"See this rod, young man? This is the very latest in trout fly rods, an absolute masterpiece, the result of years of painstaking technological research. Very expensive, mind you!"

The man's pomposity was largely lost on Charlie, accustomed as the latter was to the down-to-earth language of the glen and the unequivocal English of its school. In any case, he had eyes only for the gem in question. He had never seen such a beautiful piece of workmanship in all his young life.

"And this reel! Engineering perfection. Works as smooth as silk. Even sounds harmonious." And he pulled off some line to give auditory proof of his claim.

Again, Charlie's eyes popped. But the child had been too well brought up and was of too honest and good a nature to experience anything akin to envy.

Then out came a box which must have contained well over 100 trout flies, or at least objects which vaguely looked like trout flies. They embraced some of the more colourful known patterns - and many others, all incredibly garish and "invented" by the great Whittaker himself. These were still unknown to the angling world at large, but according to their creator, they would be universally acclaimed as soon as their undoubted superiority was appreciated. They would ensure that the name "Whittaker" would go down in the annals of angling alongside such greats as Walton and Skues, Veniard and Walker. In fact, he would be remembered long after these mortals, lesser than he, had been shrouded and forgotten in the mists of time.

Again, Charlie hardly heard his outpourings of verbal diarrhoea. He just stood there and blinked, having never seen such a massive concentration of dazzling and varied colours, except perhaps in shots of night-time Las Vegas shown on the school's coloured TV. And he was quite sure, from what he had already learned, that the sight of any one of them would have chased any self-respecting trout away up or down the burn. Even a "daft" one would fall far short of being so stupid as to accept one of these horrors.

Charlie felt he had to say something:

"Well, sur, if ye have a' this great tackle, ye must catch an awfu' lot o' troot."

"Yes, my boy, I do at home - in the South of England - but I find that up here the trout do not seem to appreciate my wonderful inventions. It's because their tastes are not refined enough, born and bred as they are in this wild country. They are not in the least educated."

"No' in the least daft, ye mean. Anyway, hoo dae ye educate a troot? Mr. Fraser has a hard enough job wi' us at the school, an' we're supposed tae have mair brains than a troot!"

In spite of his tender years, Charlie was already quite well versed in the ways of the world and was not slow to recognise either hot air or empty ostentation. Brought up under roofs, both paternal and scholastic, where the basic teaching was permeated with good sense, its aim being to foster the ability to be able to distinguish between the intrinsically good and the inherently bad, neither was he without native intelligence, and already possessed a core of that rare commodity called common sense. And he knew how to catch trout, having been well mentored by his recently deceased grandfather, absorbing from him the basic truth that something which delights the human eye need not necessarily be as attractive to a trout and suspected, as he had been told, that every season more anglers were bagged than fish, that the tackle industry made a fortune out of useless paraphernalia which was bought on a huge scale, all of which just went to prove the pathetic gullibility of the human race in general and of the angling fraternity in particular. Cheap, flashy ornaments, zany clothes, tasteless decor, trashy souvenirs, utra-fancy flies - they were all irrefutable evidence of the same disease.

All this raced through his young mind. He felt he had to enlighten Mr. Whittaker, but wasn't quite sure how to go about it:

"Ye're no' catchin' the troots we have here because oor troots are no' daft. Hoo dae ye expect them tae tak' yin o' thae things? Ye never see them on the heather or landin' on the water." He knew he was saying just what his granddad would have said.

"Impertinent little imp," thought Whittaker. "Youngsters exude too much damned confidence these days, have far too much to say for themselves. They think they know everything, even those up here in this wilderness." But instead of saying anything, he simply scowled his displeasure. Then, from Charlie:

"Well, A'm awa' tae try ma worms."

"Pooh!" grimaced Whittaker, "Worms! What's the world coming to? They shouldn't be allowed. Everyone should be made to fish fly. Nothing else."

Charlie wondered how he could be expected to do that with his misshapen old greenheart and grating reel. Then he departed, taking a known short-cut to one or two of his favourite poolets upstream. Whittaker headed straight down the main path, convinced that superiority must triumph in the end, that things could not go on as they had been doing, that to-day the trout were bound to fall over themselves in their haste to get to his infallible flies.

His three tiny, multi-coloured monstrosities - for despite their size that was an apt description - tied on No. 16 hooks and attached to 1 lb. nylon, were cast into raging white water. A hawk, hovering a foot above it, would scarcely have seen them. In any case, no trout with any sense ever lay in such turbulence.

Wee Charlie was also engaged where there were rapids, but he let his worm work its way leisurely down through the eddies close to the side. He got two fish, 6 oz. and 8 oz. Then down he went to the next deep hole, where he landed one of just under $3/4$lb. And so it went on. Arriving back at his starting point, he had nine in all, including a large-spotted beauty of just over 1 lb. It was his best catch for many a day. In fact after his fifth fish he had decided that his little bag was not big enough, and had cut a willow stick and threaded all the trout through it by their gills. He was just tying the stick to the bar of his bike when the maestro arrived, utterly disconsolate and not a little peeved.

Charlie's body at first obscured his catch.

"A blank again! These damned Highland trout! Just as I said - they're totally uncivilised. They don't know what's good for them."

Charlie was mentally quick enough to note the utter absurdity of this last remark, but was content to reply:

"I widnae say that, mister." And, stepping a little to one side, he revealed his catch.

"Good Lord! Did you catch these this afternoon?"

"Aye."

"With the worm?"

"Aye."

"My God! And they completely ignored my choicest flies!"

"Mebbe because they didnae want them? Look, Mister, I mebbe dinnae ken aboot places doon in England but I ken hoo tae fish this burn. Ma grandpa showed me."

Whittaker was hardly listening. He had suddenly seen a possible way of extricating himself from a very embarrassing situation, a way of not only saving his ego but of bathing in an aura of adulation that very evening in the hotel bar - and at breakfast before his departure.

"Eh, these fish, my boy. Could I buy them from you?"

"Whit fur?"

"Because I'm off home tomorrow morning and I would like to take them with me for some friends who adore fresh trout."

"I didnae mean that. I mean, hoo much money will ye gie me fur them?"

"Oh, I see. Eh, let's say £1?" Strange, thought Charlie, that someone who lavished so much money on fishing equipment should be so stingy when it came to evaluating the end-product of another's endeavours in the same sphere.

"£1? Nothin' doin'! There's between fower an' five pund there an' ma ma' says they're sellin' in the shops doon in Grantown at £1.60 the pund." And he immediately added:

"An' no' as fresh as mine!"

"Well, let's say £3."

"£3? Naw, £5." Charlie was perspicacious enough to observe that the man was more than a little keen to make a deal.

"£5... Well, all right!"

The trout and the money exchanged hands. Charlie had never felt so rich and his face glowed with excitement. Now he had the wherewithal, with the pound or two he had saved in his money-box, to buy that attractive second-hand rod he had seen in the shop in Grantown. The tackle-dealer had told him it could be used to fish fly as well.

But, as he cycled home, he was not so sure. What had that man achieved with his splendid equipment? And what had he himself done with his twisted but trusted old greenheart and box of worms? Anyway, according to what his granddad had told him, the burn had always been a better worm than a fly water. He would keep his money. Perhaps he would need it later on when he graduated to the big river, as his granddad had said he would some day. But the greenheart and he were regular companions who had conquered together on numerous occasions and struck up a perfect partnership. Dissolving it would be nothing short of treachery, like dropping an old and loyal friend. He couldn't even contemplate the thought of going off to the burn without it.

Charlie was affluent all right.

"X" Years Hence?

RALFO chewed his lunch as he fished on. In any case it was a relatively simple matter to extract a couple of hunger and thirst quenching pills from the capsule attached to his fishsuit by an ornamental spring clip and pop them into his mouth - no need to lay down one's rod and rummage about for things they had called thermos flasks and sandwiches in some musty old books he had found in the basement of the city library.

As he chewed, he pressed the small button on his 3 ft. long rod with his thumb and the almost invisible gossamer-thin monofilament shot out at fantastic speed. As the uncrushable insect-like lure, containing a tiny motor, hit the surface of the water, the slack was immediately taken up and the gaudy creature began to execute aquabatics all over the pool, the monofilament shortening and running out as predetermined by the setting on a little lever above the push button. Nothing else could be seen of the reel - as it had been called in bygone days - the rest of the mechanism being concealed inside the six-inch rod butt.

Ralfo felt a playful pluck and the line automatically tightened into the fish. The ultra-sharp, treble-barbed hooks took their customary hold and the tension adjusted itself as required. The very short rod remained almost rigid but this was of no consequence, the line being almost unbreakable.

The great trout, weighing 20 kilos, one of the breed produced after long years of experiment by eminent pisciculturists to replace *salmo salar* of the natural history books, had no chance to use its flabby weight and what little strength it possessed. Within 15 seconds it lay dead on the gravel, the finishing blow having been delivered by means of the two-inch bolt gun young Ralfo always carried in his fishkit.

Footsteps on the gravel made him turn round. It was an old man, gnarled and slightly bent, but fresh of face and with a twinkle in his eye. Ralfo was sure it was the oldest man he had ever seen, older even than his great-great-great grandfather who had died five years before.

"Good-day, my boy. That is quite a big fish you've caught. I would say it is in the region of 20 kilos."

"Yeah, yeah," answered Ralfo. "It's a spankler of a trutta, senior. I put him at that myself!"

"Yes, its size reminds me of the beautiful salmon I used to catch in this very pool." A long, lost look spread across the old man's face, then he went on: "I remember the very day the last recorded Atlantic salmon to be seen by man was taken in the nets off the estuary of this very river."

"You mean, senior, I talk to you who has actually seen a salmon? I have of course read of them in books but you are the first homo I meet who has eyed one."

Tales of Fishing and Fishermen

"Yes, I can see now a 28-pounder, my last big fish caught a few years before they disappeared altogether - I took it upstream from 'The Firs' - you know it as Section X2. It came as a glorious and fitting finale to the great days I had enjoyed with Atlantic salmon. You know, my boy, you could stand on this very spot and watch these magnificent fish, steel-blue of back and with bellies of pure silver - no picture or photograph has ever done them full justice - frolicking in the tail there before setting off again upstream. Those were wonderful days! What pleasure *salmo salar* gave us! He was wild and immensely strong and you had to play him till..."

"What you mean "wild"? What you mean "play" him?"

The old man did his best to explain.

"And what occurred then to finish their coming? Is it as I have read?"

"Yes, the greed of men and a horrifying disease combined forces to make the Atlantic salmon disappear from the face of the earth. But it was mainly the greed of men." He shook his head sadly, staring down at the stones. "What a tragedy. *He* was a fish!"

Ralfo looked dubious and the old man stalked away, muttering to himself.

Ralfo went on fishing, the only way he knew, fishing for the super-trout which, thanks to the scientists. had been blown up fat and stodgy to act as a substitute for the sleek, firm salmon of which the old man had spoken.

But, Ralfo mused, old people always talked like that, always making out how much better things had been in *their* time.

"Sentimental old foolies," he muttered, taking out another pill to pop his dessert course into his mouth.

Amen

FOR SOME TIME the staunch devotees of the little northern congregation had not been too happy about the piscatorial slaughter wrought by their minister, the Reverend Tom Connachie. Tom, red-faced, stockily-built and with a more colourful tongue than one normally expects to find in a churchman, had shrugged off the embarrassed but undisguised disapproval of the more forthright members of his flock. Surely it was blatantly wrong, they argued, that any human being should derive pleasure from torturing and killing innocent creatures. When the culprit was a Minister of the Church, it was no less than evil, no less than a cardinal sin.

Those who felt most strongly about the situation more or less browbeat their more tolerant (or less courageous) fellow-worshippers into action. At a secret meeting it was decided that Tom's position had become untenable and he would be asked to go. He would be told this was the wish of the majority, and hence the only practicable course.

In fact the need did not arise. One August morning, while fishing the rocky pool whose turbulent waters thundered beneath the road bridge at the entrance to the village, Tom lost his footing while trying to hold on to a wildly panicking salmon and was swept off to another kingdom.

The initial shock and the condolences expressed to Mrs. Connachie were soon replaced by talk revealing the conviction on the part of many that God himself had punished Tom for the sadistic and unpardonable pleasure he had derived from his maltreatment of the denizens of their beautiful little river. He had been taken from their midst and from his calling because he had done great wrong. They had been right and were not slow to broadcast it far and wide. What was more, God had set an example and given a dire warning.

The anglers in the congregation began to steal to the most remote parts of the river, praying that their presence there would not be noticed, but fingers were pointed and tackle was gradually laid aside.

The Kirk Session met to consider the applications for the vacancy and voted unanimously for the Reverend Jonathan Pennywhistle, who impressed them above all with his reputation for the unremitting war he waged to put an end, for ever, everywhere, to each and every form of blood-sport. And fishing was high on his list.

The Reverend Jonathan Pennywhistle was in more ways than this the antithesis of the Reverend Tom Connachie. A heaven-reaching 6 ft. 4 in., and about as broad as a good stout salmon rod, he was all any devout congregation could ask for, the epitome of rectitude and godly behaviour. In fact when the sun shone at a certain angle through the stained glass window a saintly glow seemed to emanate from his hairless crown.

Amen

It was one windy morning the following autumn that the Reverend Jonathan Pennywhistle, leaving the village to drive up to a hillside cottage to console a sick old man, ran into a pine branch which had fallen directly into his path, causing him to lose control and crash through the fence beside the bridge.

He was thrown into the pool and swept away, away to another kingdom.